Anna Louisa Hildebrand

Western Lyrics

Anna Louisa Hildebrand
Western Lyrics
ISBN/EAN: 9783744775694

Printed in Europe, USA, Canada, Australia, Japan

Cover: Foto ©Thomas Meinert / pixelio.de

More available books at **www.hansebooks.com**

Western Lyrics.

BY

ANNA LOUISA HILDEBRAND,

(A. L. H.)

DUBLIN:
McGLASHAN & GILL, UP. SACKVILLE STREET;
LONDON: SIMPKIN, MARSHALL & CO.;
EDINBURGH: J. MENZIES & CO.

1872.

DUBLIN:
PRINTED BY W. J. ALLEY AND CO.,
RYDER'S ROW, CAPEL STREET.

DEDICATION.

FRIEND of my happy youth, whose tender smile
   Was my best guerdon in the days gone by,
If that departed spirits for a while
   May stoop to us, poor mortals 'neath the sky,
I would now dedicate with tears to thee
These flow'rets gathered from fond memory.

Take them, oh friend, thou wert my teacher first
   In poesy's divinest, noblest art.
It was thy sweet companionship which nurst
   The infant germs within me, and my heart
Goes back in tender musing to the days
When that my new-born Muse first won thy praise.

Take them, they are the better part of me,
    They are the untrained breathings of my soul,
Aught in me fair or pure I give to thee.
    As backward from life's cave the stone I roll,
The world may scoff at them and me, but I
Have that within which 'bove it lifts me high.

And when my name from its great roll departs,
    And low beneath its dust my body lies,
If that my simple songs can touch some hearts,
    And dim with thoughtful tears some gentle eyes,
Methinks 'twill gladden me to feel thy name
Was interwoven close with my poor fame.

A. L. H.

PREFACE.

As with many hopes and fears a mother commits her first-born to the great ocean of life, so do I commit this volume of poems, the first-born of my soul and of my heart, to the sea of public opinion. I know that to a critical eye many faults will be evident in the following verses. My love for them, though great, is not so blind as not to be fully alive to this; but they have been my earliest friends, the companions of my thoughtful moments, the solace of lonely hours, the comforters of dark days—therefore, I hold them dear, and, therefore, I strive to win for them a place, however humble, however retired, in the grand edifice which the heads and hearts of noble-minded men and thoughtful, tender women have erected in our midst. The literature of a country is its noblest monument; and to be permitted to add even a pebble to the pile is an honour I, humble though I be, aspire to. If failure in this hope is to be my doom, let the critic pause ere he condemn me to the torture of his lash, for to quote the words of the author of "Endymion"—"There is no fiercer punishment than the failure of a great object."

A. L. H.

Turlough, Castlebar,
  Co. Mayo.

CONTENTS.

	Page.
A Connemara Girl	97
A Child's Questions	110
A Defence of Woman	27
A Happy Home	42
A Greeting and Farewell	50
A Good Woman	121
A Friendly Greeting	190
A Legend of the Middle Ages	45
A Remembrance	102
A Retrospect—Sold	170
A Slanderer Rebuked	81
A Woman of Fashion	100
All Things Must Die	20
Allan and Bessie	32
All for Love, or, the World Well Lost	92
An Old Song	75
An Invocation	105
By the Fire	14
Betrayed	73
By the Hope Within Me Springing	109
Broken Vows	155
Christmas Day, 18—	39
Church of St. Nicholas, Galway	117
Cornelia	142
Consolation	178
Chance Meetings	188
Dean Kirwan's Last Charity Sermon	186

	Page.
Echoes	30
Emmet's Capture	128
Erin, My Country	136
Eleanore's Picture	172
Edith's Sacrifice	183
Frozen to Death	15
Free	82
Fairy Land	147
Fleeting	148
Home	13
Home From the Wars—"Disfigured"	18
Historic Kisses	27
Home Sickness	66
In Memoriam	53
Incorruptible Treasure	62
Invocation to the Muse	94
Ida's Faith	179
Kylemore Lake	86
Life's Lessons	70
Love *versus* Fame	149
Leonore	159
My Alice	17
My Colleen	40
Maclise's Last Painting	52
Mabel's Lovers	77
My Star	153

CONTENTS.

	Page
No Man Hath Hired Us	127
No Irish Need Apply	166
Our Blind Child	72
Out of Danger	104
Our Little Princess	152
Peaceful Evenings	151
Remorse	183
Rosamond's Bower	139
Stella's Epitaph	26
Spring Flowers	41
Song	49
Spirit Music	55
Sir Philip Sidney	93
Sucked Oranges	116
The Eagle and the Dove	7
The Maid and the Rose	21
The Sicilian Mother's Lament for her Daughter	22
Time Brings Roses	24
The Hidden Wound	25
The Lovers	29
The Huguenot Lovers	31
The Blind Man's Bride	44
The Haven of Rest	51
To One Beloved	57
The Forsaken	58

	Page
The Letter-Box	60
The Burial of Napoleon in Paris	64
True Fortitude	67
The Haunted Mind	68
The Waves' Replies	76
The Escape	83
Turning Over the Leaves	87
To A. M. H. on her 17th Birthday	90
To — on R — Weeping	96
The Post Bag	107
The Turlough River	112
The Muse's Defence on Hearing Her Contemned	122
The Devil's Holiday	125
The Old Story	131
The Way of the World	134
To a Sea Bird	143
Through Evil Report	146
The Approach of Summer	156
The Grave of Balfe	163
The Spectre Bridegroom	173
The Ballad of Effie Burton	175
The Turning of the Tide	187
Woman's Rights	168
Union is Strength	119
"Vae Victis"	98

"Western Lyrics."

THE EAGLE AND THE DOVE.

COME rest thee, beside this river,
  And sing me that plaintive air,
While I watch thy starry eyes peeping
  Thro' the clouds of thy silken hair.

And I will forget my sorrows,
  And my spirit will glide along
As this stream thro' the fragant meadows,
  On the wings of thy sweet old song.

And 'twill waft me back to the springtide,
  That in visions I behold;
'Twill turn dim eyes to sapphires,
  And silver locks to gold.

'Twill banish the scars and furrows
  From many an aching brow;
'Twill call back the vanished faces
  That are dust in the churchyard now.

Yes, sing me the song of my childhood,
    That I learned at my mother's knee,
In each pause of thy tender music
    I will catch the deep voice of the sea.

I will hear its waves repeating
    In tender and tuneful tone,
The burden of that old ballad
    Which around my heart has grown.

'Twas the tale of a lordly eagle
    Who had wooed a forest dove,
To share his lofty eyrie
    And yield her heart's deep love.

But she told him she was not worthy,
    That no fitting mate was she
For him in his power and beauty;
    That her home was a greenwood tree.

But he came in the early morning,
    And he came in the twilight grey,
And at last to his rocky fortress
    He bore the sweet dove away.

But her soul was sick within her
    For the bowers of her forest home,
And ever her eyes were turning
    Away o'er the salt sea's foam.

And ever above the thunders
    That shook her cloud-capt nest,
She heard the song of the woodlands
    In their rustling raiment drest.

Then day by day she faded,
    And day by day she sighed
For the home of her snowy sisterhood,
    Who in leafy coverts hide.

The voice of her lordly lover,
   Or the kingly love he gave,
Could not still her spirit's yearning—
   But wherefore so pale and grave?

Does it grieve thee to think, one evening
   When the waves 'neath the sun blushed red,
In the home where her lord had borne her
   The forest dove lay dead?

Ah, child, would'st thou know the meaning
   Of this quaint old tale I tell?
Nay, turn not thine eyes from me, Ethel,
   Methinks thou knowest it well.

And he of the stately presence,
   And he of the eagle eye,
Whom yester eve in the gloaming
   I saw passing our dwelling by,

In whose veins the blood of monarchs
   With quickened tide doth flow,
Must not pluck our one sweet violet
   To twine round his lordly brow.

Why does he covet the flow'ret,
   That low by the wayside grows,
When within his pleasaunce stately
   Blooms many a queenly rose.

Bethink thee, child of the eyrie,
   Of the eagle's woodland mate;
Bethink thee of one who watches
   E'en now, by the garden gate.

He has loved thee from thy childhood,
   No belted knight is he;
But the heart that beats in his bosom
   Is true as heart may be.

And better the woodman's cottage,
    Better an honest name,
Than the silken couch of a noble,
    And a heritage of shame.

Now hie thee to thy chamber,
    The wind blows cold and chill:
Long since in his car of glory
    Sank the sun behind the hill.

And when to-night thou'rt saying
    Thy prayers by thy quiet bed,
Bethink thee, child, of the eyrie
    Where the forest dove lay dead.

*   *   *

*   *   *   *

'Twas night, but no moon was shining
    In thro' the lattice pane,
When the maiden rose from her pillow,
    While her tears fell fast as rain;

And with footsteps light as the snowflake
    That floats thro' the midnight air;
Like a shadowy ghost from a churchyard,
    She stole down the creaking stair.

And out into the darkness
    With lapwing's haste she sped;
Then paused as she reached the covert,
    To list for her warrior's tread.

A moment, and crushing the fern leaves,
    With eager steps he came,
And bent on the shrinking maiden
    His eyes of ardent flame.

And swept back the veiling tresses,
   Her sweet young face to see;
But e'er he could clasp her to him
   She sank down on her knee.

"My Lord, I have sinned deeply,
   The eagle's no mate for the dove—
To-night they told me a story—
   A story of hapless love.

"They told me of shame and sorrow,
   They told me of doom and death;
Nay, seek not to raise me fondly,
   Here will I breathe my last breath."

"Now by the Holy Virgin,
   And by mine ancient name,
Methinks thou hast grown fickle—
   As fickle as courtly dame.

"What aileth thee, little Ethel,
   That thou ravest thus to-night?
S'death, girl, thou shak'st like an aspen,
   And thy cheek is ashen white.

"Here on the heart that loves thee,
   Mine own sweet flow'ret rest;
May the foul fiend blast the babbler
   That has tortured thy timid breast.

"Does not love make all men equal?
   And what is my wealth to me,
If 'neath my castle's rooftree
   No shelter is found for thee?

"Now by mine ancient lineage,
   And by my father's sword,
By the knightly faith of the warrior
   Who never broke plighted word,

"This hand that thine is clasping
  In honour thine doth hold.
Aye, cling closer, little trembler.
  Deem not I think thee bold."

May God in his mercy shield them,
  These lovers fond and true;
For e'en now thro' the wood's green tresses
  A wingèd arrow flew.

And o'er his faithful bosom
  Her pure blood spouted red—
In the arms of her lordly lover,
  The forest Dove lay dead.

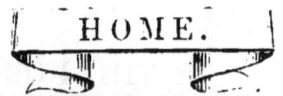

HOME.

An humble room, but rich to me,
As tho' with silken broidery
    Its walls were hung;
Not e'en the palaces of kings
Have in them two more precious things
    Their gems among.

It holds my all, this little place,
A gentle woman's winsome face
    With feeling lit;
The index to the tender heart
On which, methinks, the largest part
    Has my name writ.

And, if you look, you well can see
Something reposing on her knee
    Her child and mine.
Our one wee lamb, our pure pale pearl,
Our darling little baby girl,
    With eyes divine.

Her mother's eyes, so dark, so deep,
So wond'rous, waking from her sleep.
    Sweet wife let me
Just kneel beside thee for awhile,
And watch her happy dimpling smile
    Regarding thee.

Which is the dearer; she or thou?
Ah, love that I can never know,
    I only feel
That thou, sweet child, and thou, sweet wife
Are both far dearer than my life
    As thus I kneel.

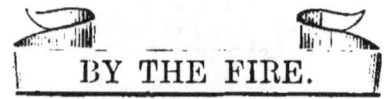

BY THE FIRE.

WITHOUT 'tis bleak and bitter cold
    A wild and stormy night,
But sit thee here my own sweetheart,
    Here in the warm firelight—
The warm firelight, my own sweetheart,
    The blessèd warm firelight.

Hark! how the sullen thunder peals,
    How loudly booms the sea!
But closer cling to me sweetheart
    Still closer unto me.
Closer to me, my own sweetheart,
    Still closer unto me.

How sweet to look in those dear eyes,
    To know them answering mine:
To feel my burning soul, sweetheart,
    Is echoed back by thine.
Is echoed back by thine, sweetheart,
    Is echoed back by thine.

We have not much of worldly gear,
    But better far than gold
Is true fond love, my own sweetheart,
    That is not bought nor sold.
That is not bought nor sold, sweetheart
    That is not bought nor sold.

In storm or calm we'll ever keep
    Our guiding star in sight,
And to life's close may we, sweetheart,
    Love as we love to-night.
Here in the warm firelight, sweetheart,
    The blessèd warm firelight.

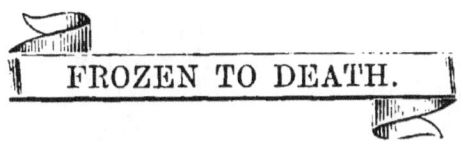

FROZEN TO DEATH.

[In Sir Leopold McClintock's Artic Expedition the body of a young Spaniard was found in the ice in a state of perfect preservation.]

HE lies not asleep 'neath his sunny vines
   Or his fragrant orange bowers,
The budding spring will ne'er deck his grave
   With all its wealth of flowers.

No loving footsteps will ever break
   That slumberer's repose;
For he lies on the shores of the frozen main
   Where the icy north wind blows.

No cross erected by pious hands
   A watch o'er his grave will keep,
No maiden will come in the dewy eve
   Beside his couch to weep.

For him was no mournful death wail sung,
   No funeral masses said,
In the loving breast of our mother earth
   His form will ne'er be laid.

For he sleeps, he sleeps, and nor prayers nor tears
   Can break his profound repose;
He lies on the shores of the frozen main,
   Where the icy north wind blows.

A robe of snow was his winding sheet,
   His winding sheet and grave,
His masses were sung by the whisp'ring sea,
   In many a far off cave.

The lovely stars of a polar night
  Were the tapers round his bed ;
He slept his last sleep with a pillow of ice
  Beneath his weary head.

The cold north winds sang his lullaby,
  As round his couch they crept,
And the moon was the only mourner there
  To watch him as he slept.

He had laid him down in the soft soft snow,
  And in thought he was at home,
He had 'scaped from his dreary solitude,
  He had crossed the ocean's foam ;

He stood 'neath the vine clad hills of Spain,
  He saw his cottage door,
Then softly softly he sank to sleep
  To awaken nevermore.

Oh! mother, mother, that keepest watch,
  Still waiting from day to day,
Go not at morn to the Holy Well,
  To our Lady's grace to pray.

Oh, maiden fix not thy longing eyes
  For ever on the sea,
He cometh not back, he cometh not back,
  He will never come back to thee.

For he sleeps, he sleeps, and nor prayers nor tears
  Can break his profound repose,
He lies on the shores of the frozen main,
  Where the icy north wind blows.

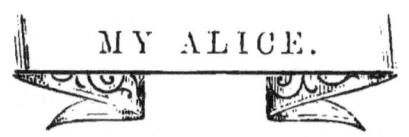

MY ALICE.

MY sister, my soul's love, my darling, my own,
    I am parted from thee and my heart feels alone,
I yearn, but in vain, for thy sweet winsome face,
And I long for the touch of thy tender embrace.
                      My Alice!

I can see thee before me, thy dark braided hair,
That droops like a cloud o'er thy forehead so fair,
And thy lovelighted eyes, that like stars shining out,
Fling a shower of glory and radiance about.
                      My Alice!

Yet it is not thy beauty, my darling, I prize,
Not thy rose tinted mouth nor thy silken fringed eyes.
'Tis the soul and the heart that so truly can speak,
In thy eloquent glance and thy swift changing cheek.
                      My Alice!

'Tis the feeling, the rapture, that of thy warm heart,
With its pulses all fire, my life has a part,
That whatever my sins or my shortcomings be,
I am sure of fond pity and pardon from thee.
                      My Alice!

Oh! girl of my blessing and girl of my prayers,
In this cold world of sorrow and sighing and tears,
In this wilderness path that thy dear feet must tread,
May the rainbow of promise hang over thy head.
                      My Alice!

My love is but weakness, but better than mine
Is the love that God gives thee, that ever is thine.
Bethink thee my dear one, whatever the gloom,
We look for a better and happier home.
                      My Alice!

Now farewell my own love, keep ever my place,
I hold thee to-day in my spirit's embrace ;
And thou, ne'er forget me when years have gone by,
And time steals life's music to leave but its sigh.
       My Alice !

Yes, love of my heart, when thou art grown old,
And this poor form of mine in the churchyard is cold,
And this voice that's now speaking is silent and still,
May a mem'ry of me give thy bosom a thrill,
       My Alice

———oo———

HOME FROM THE WARS—"DISFIGURED."

SUMMER in the sunshine,
 Summer in the air,
Summer in my bosom,
 Summer everywhere,
Why ? because she loves me,
 She will not despise
All these scars and seamings,
 Dearer in her eyes.

Shrunk I from the meeting,
 Feared to seek her door,
Lest one glance should tell me
 Everything was o'er.
But my darling clasped me
 Closer to her breast,
And on my scarred forehead
 Tender kisses prest.

Said I was her hero,
    Chid me for my fears,
Stroked my empty coat-sleeve,
    'Dewed it with her tears;
Brought the softest pillows,
    Made me lie quite still,
Said she was my captain,
    I should do her will.

Said that since I left her,
    Light had left the day;
'Tis a way with women,
    Such a winning way.
God for ever bless her,
    God for ever spare
Her who makes my summer,
    Summer everywhere.

ALL THINGS MUST DIE.

ALL things must die, so saith the proverb olden,
   Yet to the sad refrain I make reply,
Write thou the glorious truth, each word is golden,
   Deep in men's hearts, some things can never die.

The whispered word of trust and fond affection,
   The lofty musing in the thoughtful hour,
The glance that was the upright soul's reflection,
   The song that nerved our failing hands to power;

The record of some vict'ry o'er temptation,
   The generous impulse and the purpose high,
The noble deed, the spirits glad elation—
   These things can never fade, can never die.

Dust must return to dust, the grave must cover
   What most we value from our yearning eye,
Low lies the child, the father, husband, lover,
   All that is mortal must decay and die.

But fadeless and undying, the glad spirit
   Flings off the fetters that upon it weighed,
And in that world which patient souls inherit,
   Nothing shall ever die, or change, or fade.

THE MAID AND THE ROSE.

HOW chill and cold,
    Widely unrolled,
Cloud banners float athwart the sky,
    And on her bed
    The rose lies dead,
Who poured her soul out in a sigh.

    Oft in these bowers,
    In byegone hours,
She to the breezes sweets has poured,
    But now their breath
    Chills her to death,
And slays the beauty they adored.

    E'en so the maid
    Whose hopes are laid
Upon the shrine of traitor's faith;
    His love once past
    Droops i' the blast
And withers, like the rose, to death.

THE SICILIAN MOTHER'S LAMENT FOR HER DAUGHTER.

FROM THE ORIGINAL.

HERE she lies my little daughter,
    Maiden fair of fifteen years ;
Christ unto himself has caught her,
    But all fastly flow my tears.
When I see her thus before me,
A chill agony comes o'er me.

With her tresses all unbraided,
    In her richest robes arrayed,
Save that her rose cheek has faded,
    None could dream death's hand had laid
His dread signet on her brow,—
Ah, my girl, where art thou now ?

Born wert thou for bowers celestial,
    Thou our queenly radiant rose !
Thou wouldst droop 'neath skies terrestrial
    Where the wintry tempest blows.
Stolen awhile from Paradise,
Now thou seek'st thy native skies.

As the moon the stars outshineth
    Thou all others didst outshine.
Many a heart in sorrow pineth,
    Grief is not alone in mine.
I have seen full many an eye
Brighten as thy form drew nigh.

THE SICILIAN MOTHER'S LAMENT.

In the holy chapel kneeling
   I have watched their hearts grow faint;
While the fading sunlight stealing
   Down o'er sculptured nun and saint,
Filling all the sacred place,
Flung a glory on thy face.

I have seen the red blood flushing
   To thy modest downcast brow,
All the pure stream swiftly rushing,
   Crimsoned the fair front of snow,
As their glances met thine eye,
As thine ears caught each fond sigh.

Who will now console or cheer me?
   Thou my only hope art gone,
When I call who now will hear me,
   I must ever be alone.
Why did God desire thee so?
Why, my daughter, didst thou go?

If I could but die and meet thee,
   Be wherever now thou art,
Hear thy sweet voice once more greet me,
   Clasp thee to my aching heart,
If I could but find the shore
Where I ne'er should lose thee more.

Child I know thou art in Heaven,
   Kneel thee ever at God's feet,
'Till thou hear'st the summons given
   And the swift-winged angels fleet
Bear me to a perfect rest
In the mansions of the blest.

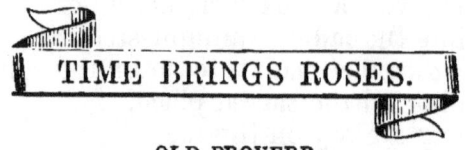
TIME BRINGS ROSES.

OLD PROVERB.

DARKNESS changeth into light,
    Trials turn to treasure,
Heaviness endures a night,
    Dawn brings pleasure.

Flowers bud from rotting leaves,
    Joys chase sorrow,
He, to-day, who groans and grieves
    Smiles to-morrow.

Bitter is the proffered cup,
    Wild the wailing,
But be brave and drink it up
    Heart ne'er failing.

Cowards only turn and fly,
    Brave men strength discover;
Sweet the smile that hides the sigh,
    Anguish masking over.

Grasp your nettle, 'twill not sting,
    Grasp it boldly, brother,
Be o'er circumstance a king,
    Vain repining smother.

Darkness changes aye to light,
    Trials turn to treasure,
Heaviness endures a night,
    Dawn brings pleasure.

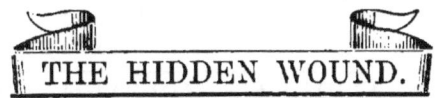

THE HIDDEN WOUND.

YOU bid me dry the foolish tears
    With which my cheeks are wet,
You tell me life has nobler aims
    Than useless vain regret,
I thank the kindly Providence
    That's done so much for me,
But there's a wound within my breast
    No eye but God's can see.

I strive to do my household work
    As it is right and meet,
I joy me in the children's talk
    And in their kisses sweet;
But when they're nestling in their beds
    And silence dwells with me,
I feel the wound within my breast
    No eye but God's can see.

I love to see the wakened earth
    Blush 'neath the rising sun,
I love to hear the lark's loud song
    That tells the day's begun;
But when the twilight's misty veil
    Falls soft o'er hill and lea,
I feel the wound within my breast
    No eye but God's can see.

When all my daily tasks are done
    I put my work away,
And kneeling down beside my bed
    I strive to think and pray;
But in the strange weird world of sleep
    Dead faces peer at me,
And oh the wound within my breast
    No eye but God's can see.

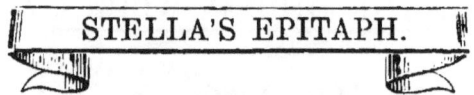

STELLA'S EPITAPH.

"ONLY A WOMAN'S HAIR."

ONLY a woman's hair,
    Only a heap of dust.
Only a life woe darkened,
    Only a murdered trust.

Only a soul troth slighted,
    Only a little token,
Only a mute memento
    Of a heart by anguish broken.

Only a world of passion
    Prest into one short hour,
Only a sweet bud blasted
    Just as it set to flower.

Only a noon of rapture
    Ending in nights of tears,
Only a wearing burden
    Borne thro' weary years.

Only a sick, sick longing,
    Only an aching care,
Only a hope deep nurtured
    Under a deep despair.

Only a love undying
    In a wild warm heart represt,
Only a dream departed,
    Only a life's unrest.

Only a ceaseless craving
  Ne'er to be satisfied,
Only a woman's passion
  Mightier than woman's pride.

Oh what a mournful story,
  Oh what a hurt laid bare,
Oh what a wail of sorrow,
  "Only a woman's hair."

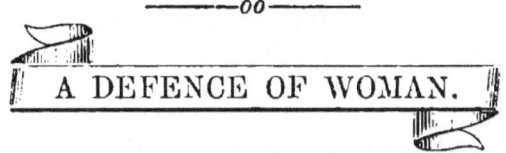

A DEFENCE OF WOMAN.

TO ONE WHO SAID ALL WOMEN WERE MERCENARY.

YOUR satire is severe yet I can't blame you,
  'Tis aimed at those who ventured to defame you,
Yet of high treason do you stand attainted,
Women are not so black as you have painted,
Tho' some to win a home and to escape
A life of toil—too often wed an ape,
Needs must when some one drives, and
                    Oh, Sir Poet,
We oft can't help ourselves and
                    Well you know it.

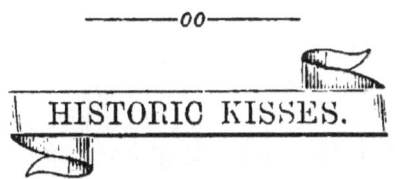

HISTORIC KISSES.

THE kiss that, on the fair and sunny brow
  Of Petrarch's Laura, once was humbly prest
By a most gallant monarch, kneeling low
  Beside the footstool of his gentle guest.

The kiss Paōlo gave a soft cheek's bloom
    Upon that day in which they " read no more ' —
Oh fatal kiss that doomed their souls to roam
    For countless ages on the Stygian Shore !

The kiss of Gauffre Rudel, Prince of Blaye,
    Who pined for love, and sailing o'er the sea
With dying haste, cast anchor in the bay
    That laves the shores of sunny Tripoli.

And when they told the Ladye of his love
    How that to death the noble prince was nigh,
She came, and pitying hung his couch above
    To feel upon her lips his latest sigh.

And then that other, precious fatal kiss
    That Raimon's wife to her fond lover gave,
So full of anguish, rapture, sorrow, bliss—
    That hurried both to an untimely grave.

There was the kiss of haughty Marguerite,
    Of which the happy poet sung so oft,
When kneeling humbly at his mistress' feet
    He felt its touch so exquisite—so soft.

The kiss that fair, ill-fated Mary gave
    The sleeping boy, in presence of her court,
She saw not then dim shadows o'er her wave,
    When she bestowed that kiss in playful sport.

Sweet is the kiss the faithful maiden gives
    To her young lover, in the Peri's tale,
For ever in our hearts that fond kiss lives,
    Mixed with the anguish of her bosom's wail.

"The last long kiss which she expires in giving,"
    When from his lips she stole the poisoned breath ;
For her no aching void, no bitter grieving,
    " Lovely in life, united in their death."

Mournful the kisses of that hapless pair
   Whose story yet can thrill us, while we read
How young they were, how faithful and how fair,
   How helpless, friendless, in their direst need.

Full of poetic fancy, to our eyes,
   Is the first kiss of her, the Night's fair queen ;
While on Mount Ida's tops Endymion lies,
   And droops she o'er him clad in silver sheen.

————oo————

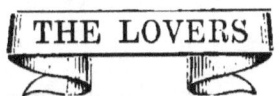

THE LOVERS

CARESSED and caressing
   She lies on his breast,
His pride and his blessing
   His dearest and best ;
Caressed and caressing
   She pillows her face
On the arms fondly pressing
   In tender embrace.

The paleness of feeling
   Is over his brow,
His spirit is kneeling
   In reverence now ;
Divine and yet human
   Half earth and half heaven
Seems blent in the woman
   Who to him is given.

The world all unheeded,
   Cheek prest unto cheek ;
No language is needed
   Their rapture to speak ;

In tremulous breathing
    The story is told,
In arms fondly wreathing
    The page is unrolled.

The angels in heaven
    Are smiling at this,
For in Eden was given
    This exquisite bliss,
And beings immortal
    Untainted by sin,
Keep watch by the portal
    That shutteth love in.

———oo———

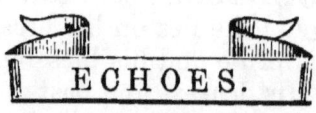

ECHOES.

(From an Arabic MS.)

THE days of my youth, oh! where are they?
    I seek, but I may not find;
They're past, like a dream of morn, away,
    Or an echo on the wind.

The voices of youth, they, too are fled,
    I seek them in many a hall,
But a dreary silence reigns instead,
    None answer to my call.

The hopes of my youth, oh! they have past,
    Like the mist from the mountain's brow,
To the winds and waves they were long since cast,
    But their memory is with me now.

I stand in the mansion my fancy made,
   No living faces there,
But many a pale and mournful shade
   Is hovering in the air.

The love of my youth, I hear a voice,
   And it shrieks to me " Lost, lost, lost,"
Oh, dream of my life! my heart's first choice,
   Art thou but a sheeted ghost ?

―――oo―――

THE HUGUENOT LOVERS.

GO! go! I will not pain thee more,
   Go from my arms and die,
See I have wiped away my tears,
   Thou shalt not hear one sigh.

Go, for thine honour unto me
   Is dearer than my life,
Away—while I am strong to bear
   The anguish and the strife.

Oh, not for me, oh, not for me,
   Shalt thou dishonoured live,
Would that for thine this life of mine
   I to the sword could give.

But tho' my heart is strong for thee,
   My woman's arm is weak,
Yet may I love thee to the last,
   And words of comfort speak.

I will pluck off this snowy scarf,
    And cast it to the flame,
Better to fill a glorious grave,
    Than live a life of shame.

Go forth, I will not keep thee back,
    My bosom's only lord!
See, I will buckle on thy spurs
    And gird thy knightly sword.

Oh, may the God of Battles shield
    Thy dear life in the fight,
Yet if thou diest I still shall know
    'Twas to defend the right.

And tho' the stroke that drinks thy blood
    My life will sever too,
Still, still, I would not have thee live
    Unto thy faith untrue.

———oo———

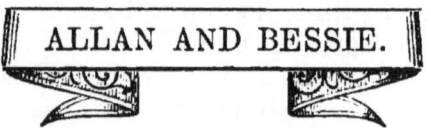

ALLAN AND BESSIE.

A Story, founded on Fact.

TWILIGHT has fallen all silently
    On the quiet village street,
No longer upon the pavement came
    The pattering of busy feet,
And loud in the old clock tower
    You could hear its great heart beat.

Silently, softly, and slowly
    The mantle of night fell down,
Away to its nest each wild-wood bird
    Had long since gladly flown,
And up from the spreading meadows
    Came the scent of the hay new mown.

In the porch of the miller's cottage
    Sat the miller's daughter fair,
The first faint beams of the moonlight
    Cast a halo on her hair,
Not a maiden in all the village
    With sweet Bessie could compare.

Not alone 'mid the roses and jessamine
    Was Bessie that summer night,
In the brown palm of Allan, the blacksmith,
    Lay her hand so soft and white,
The moon as she sailed in her glory
    Ne'er looked on a fairer sight.

Stalwart was he and handsome,
    Of all the youths the pride,
His name and his praise were spoken
    In all the country side;
Long had he loved fair Bessie
    And wooed her for his bride.

All day he had worked at his anvil,
    And he thought when that work was done,
Of how, from her father's fireside,
    To meet him his love would run,
And he blessed God for the promise
    That from her lips he'd won.

And now, as he watch'd the moonlight
    Upon her fair brow gleam,
To him as the face of an angel
    That young girl's face did seem;
Oh happy lover and maiden,
    Ye are dreaming the old old dream!

PART II.

Dream on now, happy lovers,
   This calm, sweet night in June,
Dream on now, happy lovers,
   The morn will come too soon;
"Oh not too soon," they whisper,
   While faded fast the moon.

"To-morrow," and he kissed her
   On upturned lip and brow,
"To-morrow," and he blessed her
   With tender voice and low,
Oh, fool! can any "Morrow"
   Bring half such bliss as "Now?"

"To-morrow, love, to-morrow,
   What joy to us 'twill bring!
To-morrow—When the villagers
   Our wedding bells shall ring."
He ceased—around her fondly
   His eager arms to fling.

And now he goes—yet going
   He hurries back once more
To where she still is standing,
   Within the half-closed door;
It is to whisper softly
   "To-morrow" o'er and o'er.

But then at last she bids him,
   With pretty passion, "Go,"
And from her side he parteth
   With halting step and slow,
While e'en the flowers round him
   Looked up his joy to know.

Blithe rose the morning, and blithely
   The miller's household rose,
One face new beauty borrowed
   E'en from its short repose,
And like a pearl was Bessie
   In her white wedding clothes.

Now all her young companions
   Came trouping in to see
The darling of the village,
   And in her train to be;
Oh, blest is he who claimeth
   A bride so fair as she!

They gathered round to greet her,
   They touched her hand and smiled,
The miller's eyes were misty—
   She was his only child—
While near her, ever watchful,
   Sat her dear mother mild.

"God bless you, girl, God bless you,"
   The good old miller said,
And stroked with tender fondness,
   His darling's golden head.
"God bless you and the partner
   Whom you to-day will wed."

" 'Tis time that we were going
   The Bridegroom's gone, I trow—
Who calls me? for a tumult
   Seems 'mong the people now,
And as in fright or anger,
   They're moving to and fro."

Forth strode the miller swiftly,
   And pushed the crowd aside,
"Tell me," he said, "nor strive ye
   Some cruel truth to hide
Is the Lord's hand upon us?
   Has our young Allan died?"

Not so, but they have sought for,
   And none knew aught of him;
Then fiercely swore the miller,
   And shook in every limb;
But by his side was Bessie,
   Her eyes with terror dim.

"What is it, oh, what is it?
   Oh, father is he dead?"
"Better he were, my daughter,
   They say that he has fled;"
Then like a flower broken,
   Low drooped poor Bessie's head.

And on her mother's bosom
   She like a corpse sank down,
Her soft cheek blanching whiter
   Than her white wedding gown.
"Not false, oh, no, my Allan,'
   She gasped out with a groan.

They bore her in and laid her
   Within her curtained room,
And on the miller's cottage
   Fell the silence of the tomb,
While every fireside whispered
   The tale of grief and gloom.

Days passed, but still he came not,
   Week followed after week,
And Bessie's eyes waxed dimmer,
   And paler grew her cheek,
But no word of complaining
   Her sad sweet voice did speak.

And when the miller's anger
   Broke forth in curses low,
She pressed her hands together,
   And writhed as 'neath a blow;
"Oh, father, do not curse him,
   Oh, God, it hurts me so."

Thus the dark years dragged onward
  Their dreary, doleful way,
Till in their graves together
  The good old couple lay,
And Bessie's golden tresses
  Had long since changed to gray.

Her brothers and her sisters
  Had wedded each a mate,
But still for one who came not
  She ever seemed to wait,
Still gazed she from the window,
  Still paused she at the gate.

One morn the neighbours told her,
  How miners digging deep
Had found a cold corpse lying
  Unharmed in its last sleep.
So forth she went, and softly
  To the pit's mouth did creep.

And there, as when she saw him,
  Full thirty years before,
There as when last she kissed him,
  Beside her father's door,
Lay dead her own true lover,
  Come back to her once more.

With a wild strength she struggled
  In through the surging crowd,
And then above the noises
  Her full heart shrieked aloud,
"Not false, my love, my darling,"
  And o'er the corpse she bowed.

All knew her tale, and awestruck
  The people backward stept,
The women smote their bosoms,
  Stern men in silence wept,
While quietly beside him
  She lay as tho' she slept.

Yes, quietly beside him,
　In the last sleep she lay,
Never again to waken
　Till Christ's great Judgment Day;
Parted in life, death mingles
　Within one grave their clay.

———oo———

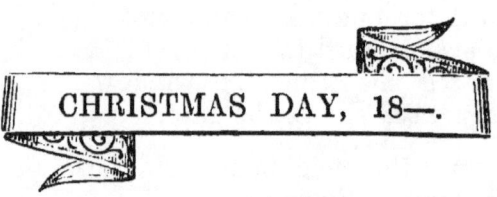

CHRISTMAS DAY, 18—.

AND this is Christmas time, but where the faces
　That made our Christmas in the days gone by?
We look around the hearth on vacant places,
　Till our faint smiling fades into a sigh.

Many a bright eye bids welcome to this morning,
　Many a young voice is carolling aloud,
All thoughs of care with gladsome laughter scorning,
　For such are there no tears, no dark rain-cloud.

And silently and softly tears are falling,
　But tears may not the lost, the loved restore,
Vainly such hearts are for their dear ones calling,
　One sad voice breaks the silence, "Nevermore."

Oh, nevermore—it is the solemn chorus,
　It is the sad refrain to earthly chimes,
Oh, never more—a mournful pall hangs o'er us,
　While memory brings us back past Christmas times.

Where are the warm hand-claspings we remember?
　Where is the welcoming look, the whispered tone?
How dull and dreary is this dark December!
　While over lonely graves the wild winds moan.

Where are the golden sunsets, where the glory
    That wrapt us in a halo sea and sky?
Oh, sad and strange is life's mysterious story,
    And vain the yearning for the long gone by.

Where are the dreamings fond we used to cherish?
    Where are the flowers we gathered long ago?
We watched our dearest dream joy fade and perish,
    We laid our best loved treasure 'neath the snow.

God's mighty hand our air-built castle shattered,
    God's mighty voice dispelled our waking dreams,
Lo! on the earth hope's brightest buds are scattered,
    Yet see a streak of light from Heaven gleams.

I hear a voice—"Be hushed your bitter crying,
    I come to pour my peace in your sad breast;
Mourn not your lonely home, your loved ones dying,
    Bethink you they are safe, they are at rest.

"Poor blinded mortal, would you keep them ever
    Still bearing the sad burden of life's care?
Will you not meet again no more to sever?
    Sad child of sorrow, I your grief can share.

"My love is everlasting—tho' I chasten
    I would not have you shed one needless tear,
Home to myself I would your footsteps hasten,
    And those you loved so well to me are dear."

MY COLLEEN.

STANDING with her pitcher,
    See my Colleen fair!
Sunny drops like diamonds
    Glistening on her hair;
Underneath their lashes
    Brighter gleam her eyes,
There are shifting glories
    Blue as summer skies.

Is there any lady,
    Of whate'er degree,
Crown'd Queen or Empress,
    Half so fair as she?
Let them count their jewels,
    Gems, and gold and pearl,
None are half so lovely
    As my Irish Girl.

Fairer is her girdle,
    Tho' 'tis hodden grey,
And her snowy 'kerchief
    Than their gewgaws gay;
Underneath that 'kerchief
    Beats a heart of gold,
And a love unmeasured
    Makes its worth untold.

Now she hears my footstep,
    Ah, that happy start
Sends the blood in torrents
    Up from her warm heart.
Has there not a brightness
    Fallen upon the place?
Yes, the sunny smiling
    Of her glowing face.

Rosy mouth uplifted,
    Would it be amiss—
How the sweet lips tremble—
    Just to snatch one kiss?
Sure she would not blame me
    When her eyes smile so?
Sweet! those eyes forgive me
    Tho' the lips say "No."

———oo———

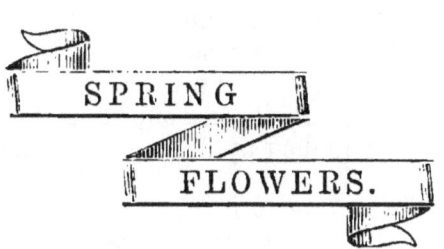

SPRING FLOWERS.

I GATHERED these flow'rets this morning,
    While night's tears on their sweet faces lay,
The hedgerow and wild-wood adorning,
    The heralds of sunshine and May.

I send them, nor fear thou'lt despise them,
    All their beauty I know *thou* wilt see,
As the children of Nature I prize them,
    They are "footsteps of angels" to me.

They are "stars of our earth," and a token
    Of a Hope ever-springing and new,
Of a Promise thro' ages unbroken,
    Of a Love never-dying and true.

Like them in the winter we perish,
    Like them close our world-wearied eyes,
But the beautiful hope we all cherish
    That, like them, from the dust we'll arise.

A HAPPY HOME.

SHUT in by loving kindness,
    By holy hills fenced round,
Far from the world's rude clamour,
    A happy home is found.
The dove of peace is brooding
    That quiet nest above,
Where life's best chords make music,
    Touched by the minstrel, Love.

There morn brings no sad waking,
    Or midnight no dread dreams,
But thro' the opened lattice
    The sun of promise gleams;
There sleep, like dews descending,
    But ope's a fairer world,
While o'er the peaceful dwelling
    God's banner is unfurled.

There children's merry laughter
    Startles the stilly air,
There Faith and Love are kneeling
    Beside their beds in prayer,
There tales of past endeavour
    The twilight hours will while
And brave man find his guerdon
    In loving woman's smile.

You've seen the forest monarch
    By graceful vine clasp'd round,
And high amid his branches
    The purple fruit you've found;

So round his manhood stately
   In beauty twineth she,
And God's own flowers are blooming
   Upon the parent tree.

Oh! proud must be the mother
   Of her three bonny boys,
What wells of hope are in them,
   What pure, untainted joys;
But nestling in her bosom
   The fairest flower is seen,
And baby is the darling,
   And baby is the queen.

The one sweet little daughter
   God to her yearning sent,
The golden rose of beauty,
   From Heaven's garden lent.
Oh, lady fair and gentle,
   True wife and mother good,
Thou wearest on thy forehead
   The crown of womanhood.

Oh, clasp thine hands in gratitude,
   And bend thy spirit's knee,
To Him who in the cup of life,
   Poured so much sweet for thee;
And when thou steal'st at midnight
   To bless thy treasures rare,
Thank God, who led thee to this fount,
   To quench thy soul's thirst there.

These are thy jewels—guard them well,
   Nor let their lustre fade,
But e'en yet lovelier may they grow
   What God so lovely made.
As He in mercy did by thee
   E'en so do thou by them,
Then polished by thy careful hand,
   Brighter shall gleam each gem.

The hills of God stand round thee,
　The hope of heaven is thine,
Christ's hand has changed the water
　Of this sad life to wine.
He fills the golden chalice
　With blessings to the brim,
Oh, while we taste His mercy
　May we remember Him.

"THE BLIND MAN'S BRIDE."

THE Blind Man's Bride, and dost thou think for me
　That there is aught of sadness in the word?
Oh, that thou were not blind, that thou could'st see
The deep deep joy that in my soul is stirred.

With me thou wilt forget that thou art blind,
For I will walk for ever at thy side,
And with the glorious vision of the mind,
Thou'lt see how blest am I, the Blind Man's Bride.

I will be eyes to thee, and I will teach
To thee the wondrous language of the earth,
For these the whispering waves will have a speech,
And thou wilt joy thee in the storm's fierce mirth.

For thee I never never shall grow old,
Others may see a dimness in my eye,
And silver where thou'lt see but threads of gold,
As thou last saw them on thy bosom lie.

I, too, will be thy guardian—at that thought
How my weak woman's heart swells high with pride;
Oh, may I love and guard thee as I ought,
And may'st thou live to bless the Blind Man's Bride.

And thou shalt see me in the world above,
Where nought of sorrow or of gloom may be,
There shall I love thee with a holier love,
Then what now darkest seems we both shall see.

A LEGEND OF THE MIDDLE AGES.

IT was a holy morn, and calm, and wrapt in vapours
  gray,
All cradled round by circling hills a peaceful valley lay,
And from the sombre forest's shade the gazer's eye might
  see
The curling smoke in columns rise from an ancient
  priory.
No sound of life the silence broke, but on the stilly air
Was heard the tuneful matin chime calling the monks to
  prayer.
And now within the ancient pile the pious brethren
  prayed,
And fervent orisons to God in reverence they made.
Down thro' the oriel window pane the morning sunlight
  poured
A flood of light on sculptured tombs, where decked with
  helm and sword
Full many a warrior's marble form in stately slumber
  lay,
While far below his crumbling dust awaits the judgment
  day.
It fell on many a lovely face of martyr and of saint,
On many a tall and sculptured arch and many a carving
  quaint ;
But with a tenderer lustre, methought the sunbeams shed
A halo round the silver locks of the prior's hoary head.

A brooding calm, a witching spell, fell o'er the sacred place,
And a light that was not of this earth beamed from his earnest face,
As lovingly he told the tale of Him, that perfect One,
Who by His death a crown of life for all His followers won.
Before him, clad in garments white, two fair-haired children knelt,
Gazing on them the sternest heart with tenderness might melt
So fair they were, so beautiful, so free from mortal stain,
They seemed not creatures of this world of sin and shame and pain;
Clad in their shining, spotless robes, their sunny tresses fell
O'er cheeks that wore the roseate hue of ocean's tinted shell,
Their meek hands folded on their breasts, their soft eyes turned to heaven,
They looked like angels who awhile unto this earth were given;
They had been orphans from their birth, a soldier was their sire,
Who, torn from his twelvemonth's bride to glut a tyrant's ire,
Fell on a distant battle-field, while she, the widowed one,
Just lived to bless her new-born babes, nor saw another sun.
The orphans are the care of God, and now his servant came
To lead them early in the way that honoureth His name,
And every morn these infants went, like Samuel of old,
To minister unto the priest as he God's page unrolled.
Soon as the sacred rites were done the holy prayers prayed,
In blessing on their golden heads his hand the prior laid,
Then bade them seek the little nook where every morning they
Sat down to eat the frugal meal which waited them always.

Once as they sat and broke their bread in peaceful quiet there,
Unseen by them approached a child of presence wondrous fair,
Heard they no sound of opening door, no tread of busy feet,
But, lo! between them at the board sat down the stranger sweet.
His was no face of mortal mould, it was too pure and bright,
And in his eyes a glory dwelt—a radiant, heavenly light—
As tenderly he talked to them, and tasted of their bread,
Then silently, e'en as he came, away he vanished.
Soon to the holy man they haste, and tell their wondrous tale,
His withered cheek flushed crimson deep, then faded ashy pale,
" Oh, children! blessèd are ye now, it was the Holy Child,
The meek, the spotless Lamb of God, the Saviour undefiled;
It was the Babe of Bethlehem who deigned your feast to bless,
When next He comes His sacred feet with kisses fond caress,
And say, e'en as you sink to earth on humble rev'rent knee,
Grant, Lord, as thou hast shared our bread, that we may sup with thee."
The children sought their simple toil, and whiled the noon away
In healthful labour and in bursts of happy boyish play,
But ever thro' the hours they longed for morning's light once more,
That they might see the wondrous face that bent their table o'er.
It came, at the appointed hour the gentle form drew nigh,
Then low they sank into the earth, with rev'rent lip and eye,
And cried, " O Lord, as thou hast shared our bread and let us see

Thy holy face, grant that in Heaven we yet may sup with
thee."
He smiled, and blessed them silently, then spake—" Oh,
infant's twain
" A little while, and this, your prayer, shall not be prayed
in vain,
" Not many suns shall o'er this earth in golden splendour
rise,
" Till you, who loved me here on earth, shall feast in
Paradise."
He ceased, then rising in the air on wings of amber light,
'Mid sweet-voiced angels' harmonies, he vanished from
their sight.
And now another day has dawned, and, kneeling at the
shrine,
Behold the altar fitly spread with sacred bread and wine;
Behold the father raise the cup—the bread all meekly
share,
Then bowed each head till he should breathe a blessing
and a prayer.
He knelt with awe-uplifted eyes, the children at his side,
The monks, with shrouded faces, thought on Him who for
them died,
And waited, with a reverent hush, the solemn words to
hear,
But lo! all dumbly there he knelt, no blessing reached the
ear.
They rose, and to the altar steps, with hasty feet they
prest,
Lifeless was he, with withered hands crost calmly on his
breast;
His spirit, summoned by his God, to Heaven had passed
away,
And death but beautified the face that now was changed
to clay.
They turned to rouse the little ones, who seemed as tho'
they slept;
Then broken was the awful spell, and loud the brethren
wept—

For dead and cold, like him they loved, lay the sweet children there,
The waiting angel had not stirred one ringlet of their hair;
And as in mute amaze each sank down on adoring knee,
A voice was heard that shook the walls of the ancient priory,
That cried—"Weep not for those who died, they sup in Heaven with Me."

SONG.

OH, strike thine harp to other themes,
    Sing not to me of love,
Athwart my soul strange glory gleams,
    Thro' brighter worlds I rove.

I tremble to my heart's deep core,
    My firmness I forget,
Away! I can endure no more
    This yearning, this regret.

Oh! if thou sing'st of love to me,
    Say 'twas unsought or crost;
It must not blest or happy be,
    For all of mine was lost.

Yet strike thy tender harp again,
    And I will choose the song;
Let every note be stored with pain,
    With agony and wrong.

Sing of a bright life darkened o'er,
    Sing of despair and woe;
But sing of happy love no more,
    There's none the Heavens below.

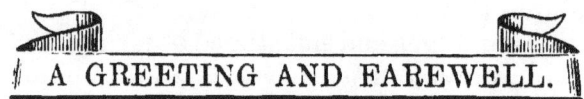

A GREETING AND FAREWELL.

COME closer comrades to the hearth,
    Let bumpers brimming be,
And we will drink the New Year's birth,
    The Old Year's memory.

The cup is mixed both sad and sweet,
    We drink with smiles and tears,
As by us Sixty-nine doth fleet,
    To join the vanished years.

He goes with bowed and silvered head,
    With footsteps faint and slow;
Ah, blithe and gladsome was his tread
    But twelve short months ago.

He came with light and laughing hours,
    He goes with mingled tears,
Faded his coronal of flowers,
    He joins the vanished years.

His work is done, but still remain,
    Tasks neither light nor few,
For us, who laughed at sorrow's chain
    When this old year was new.

We learned the lesson time will teach,
    Howe'er we may rebel,
Striving in vain the clouds to reach,
    Down to the earth we fell.

We laid some faces in the dust,
    Beneath the coffin lid,
Their souls are safe with God, we trust,
    Altho' their forms be hid.

And fair and bright the New Year stands,
    With heart and hope elate,
His buds of promise in his hands,
    Without the city gate.

The dew of youth is on his brow,
    Its glory in his eyes;
New Year we bid you welcome now
    With smiles, and yet with sighs.

For oh! the past was strangely sweet,
    And who can chide our tears
As by us Sixty-nine doth fleet
    To join the vanished years?

———oo———

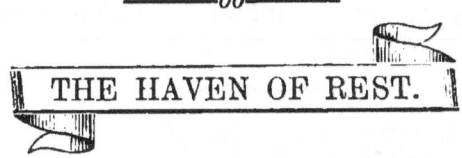

THE HAVEN OF REST.

"So he bringeth them to the haven where they would be."

I FEEL as tho', a child again, I sought my mother's breast,
And I am glad, like Israel, because I am at rest;
No more my bark is buffeted upon life's angry sea,
He has brought me to the haven where I fain would be.

The path was very thorny, the way seemed very long,
But now, from out a grateful heart, I raise a joyful song;
A strange, sweet beauty wraps me round, my panting soul is free,
For he brings me to the haven where I fain would be.

The draught was bitter at the dregs, 'twas bitter at the brim,
Yet who shall dare to curse the cup that is poured out by Him?
I cried out in my grief to God, he has delivered me,
And brings me to the haven where I fain would be.

Now out upon the cruel hearts that triumphed in my woe,
I shook your dust from off my feet, and left you long ago ;
Your bitter taunts, like venomed darts, no more may fall
  on me,
God brings me to the haven where I fain would be.

Oh, while I live His Holy Name I shall for ever bless,
He hearkened to my misery, he mocked not my distress,
His voice can chain the roaring winds, can calm the vexéd
  sea,
He brings me to the haven where I fain would be.

The haven is a loving heart within an honest breast,
'Tis there I find my happiness, 'tis there I find my rest ;
An isle of peace it rose for me out of life's troubled sea,
God bless for ever my dear home, for there I fain would be.

———oo———

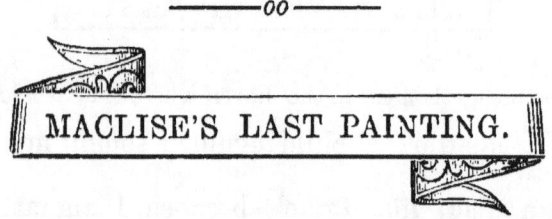

MACLISE'S LAST PAINTING.

The Geraldine borne from the field by the followers of Ormond.

THE battle had been fierce and long,
  On the red plain a mighty throng
Of dead and dying lay ;
And forth from that hard-conquered field
The victors bore upon his shield
  A vanquished chief that day.

Speechless he lay, his dark locks wet
With muddy stain and gory sweat,
  His stricken hand
Down by his side all powerless hung,
But yet his stiff'ning fingers clung
  Fast to his brand.

But tho' the blood had fled his cheek,
His flashing eyeballs still could speak,
   His spirit high;
He bore with a grim, silent smile
His captors tauntings for a while,
   Nor made reply.

But when they cried, with mocking word,
"Where art thou now, thou haughty lord?"
   Then fierce he spake—
"Where ever was the Geraldine,
And every son of his great line—
   On Butlers' necks."

IN MEMORIUM.

CHARLES DICKENS.

WE did not dream that thou could'st die,
   Who late among us moved,
We thought that death must pass thee by,
   So much, so well beloved;
But now, indeed, too well we know,
That even thee he has laid low.

Oh! friend to many a lonely heart,
   High soul and glorious mind,
Too soon from us thou did'st depart,
   Leaving no peer behind;
To fill thy place whom shall we call?
Ah! where did thy great mantle fall?

Full many a tender tear we shed
   While hanging o'er thy words,
And oh, to think that thou art dead,
   Who touched our heart's best chords;
Retreating from life's dusty road,
Thou hast cast off its weary load.

Yes, thou hast now begun "that world
  Which maketh up for this,"
The shattered ship her sail has furled
  Across death's dark abyss;
The Orient gate of Heaven lies
God knows how welcome to thine eyes.

For thou, tho' seated on a throne
  High above other men,
Perhaps some bitter griefs hast known
  Far, far beyond our ken;
Immortal and yet mortal too,
Only thy surface life we knew.

Bitter and sweet—'tis ever so,
  Yet, if thou could'st believe
With what a deep and heartfelt woe
  We o'er thine ashes grieve,
Methinks thy spirit eyes would smile,
And thy freed soul be glad the while.

We lay thee down—a nation's tear
  Thine honoured grave bedews,
Nor shall men's hearts for many a year
  Their tribute grief refuse;
Back to thy God thy life we give,
And dying know thou still shalt live.

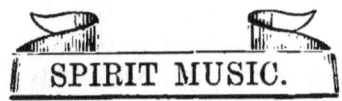

SPIRIT MUSIC.

HERE I'm sitting, ever drinking
   Long, deep drafts from fancy's bowl,
And of thee my heart is thinking,
   While strange music floods my soul.

Sweeping softly, low and faintly
   Comes this music in the night,
And a solemn rapture saintly
   Thrills me with a pure delight.

'Tis as tho', on white clouds seated,
   Sang some seraph in the air,
And the cadence is repeated,
   Round me, 'bove me, everywhere.

Down through fields of light it stealeth,
   Fields of azure and of gold,
Till my eager spirit kneeleth,
   As it were, in Heaven's fold.

And I close my eyes in slumber,
   While the angels bear my head,
Angels beauteous without number
   Bending softly o'er my bed.

When the golden arrows hovering
   Thro' the eastern window, dart
Thro' its fleshy mortal covering
   Right into my waking heart.

While each opening flower's distilling
   Perfumes fragrant to the sky,
And the song of birds is filling
   All my ear as calm I lie.

Then above the thousand voices
　　With which Nature offers praise,
Still my inmost soul rejoices
　　In her own fantastic lays.

And an unseen minstrel, sweeping
　　Golden strings, such music makes,
That a rain of happy weeping
　　From my dreamy eyelid breaks.

When at noon I'm toiling onward
　　'Neath the load all flesh must bear,
Still my soul is soaring sunward
　　To the music murmuring there.

O'er the clamour and the beating
　　On life's road of busy feet,
Still my soul thy soul is meeting
　　In a converse low and sweet.

O'er the sadness and the pleasure,
　　O'er the laughter and the sighs,
Ever breathes that tuneful measure
　　Floating downward from the skies.

Love, thou art the minstrel making
　　Sounds harmonious in my soul,
Of life's harp each chord awaking
　　Drawing music from the whole.

TO ONE BELOVED.

OH, poet soul! tho' shrined in house of clay,
    Why should'st thou weep and chide thy prison state?
Thine is the glory of undying day;
Around thee white-winged seraphs ever wait,
    To wander at thy bidding thro' the air;
Methinks their breath flings perfume everywhere.

Thou holdest converse with them, thou can'st hear
Their plaintive voices murmuring lovely things
    Of beauty and of poesy, and in thine ear
It is the songs of Heaven each minstrel sings,
    The songs of a fair world—a far-off clime—
Filled with the breath of orange flower and lime.

The songs of dreamland where, with chaplets crowned,
Upon a couch of violets, genius lies,
    Her mantle cast aside, her hair unbound,
While from her worshippers faint hymns arise;
    Soft, tuneful pœans, as, with rev'rent tread,
They scatter perfumes on her od'rous bed.

Thy soul is steeped in thought, as in a sea
Of rosy light—and as its billows stealing
    In from the boundless ocean surge o'er thee,
Each wave returning bears some spark of feeling,
    Some gem of rarest brightness from the shore
That lay deep buried in the sand before.

A world of poesy is in thine eyes,
The fount that gave them light is not of earth,
    On heavenly hills, methinks, it had its rise;
Oh, sweet child-woman! often in the dearth
    Of pity or of feeling have I prayed
On thy fond breast my head might soon be laid.

I never gazed upon a sunlit sea,
I never wandered by a rock-girt shore,
  But a vague yearning want arose in me
For thy sweet answering face, that I might pour
  Into thine earnest, listening ear a part
  Of that which swelled to breaking my full heart.

A burst of martial music—a low tune
Breathed in the solemn hush of eventide;
  A tale of fruitless love—a fading moon,
A fleecy cloud of glory rainbow-dyed,
  Aught that exalts, ennobles, purifies,
  Wins glorious tribute from thy deep dark eyes.

Like to a forest temple is thy mind,
From which the incense-breathing odours steal,
  Yielding their treasures to the wooing wind,
While round the shrine fond votaries humbly kneel;
  My fancy hath run riot—on this shrine
  No hand a garland lays, save only mine.

I see thee, and I tremble—thou wert given
Those noblest gifts of God—a poet's soul,
  And a warm human heart, which must be riven
By many a lightning shaft, until the scroll
  Of thy life's fate be read, and freed from prison
  Up to Heaven's gate thy radiant soul hath risen.

———oo———

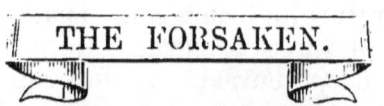

THE FORSAKEN.

I'M sitting in my lonely room,
    And watching a starlit sky,
My thoughts are with the happy past,
    The days so long gone by,
I wonder if their mem'ry wake
    Within your breast a sigh.

THE FORSAKEN.

I wonder if you ever wish
    Those days again could be,
Or have you blotted from your heart
    The faintest trace of me?
And cast my memory and my love
    Into oblivion's sea?

Alas! I know my prayers are weak,
    I know my tears are vain,
I know you have forgot the face
    That on your breast has lain;
But ah! for me this yearning want,
    This never dying pain.

Within the busy haunts of men
    You fill your wonted place;
Your step is lightsome as of yore,
    A smile is on your face;
I know, I feel, you've blotted out
    Of me the faintest trace.

They told me—but I mocked their words—
    For you I was no mate;
Ah, me! that bitter, bitter truth
    I learned, alas! too late;
Yet I have borne, and I will bear,
    The stern decree of fate.

Perchance you yet may know and feel
    What 'tis to be alone,
Perchance you yet may miss the light
    That from your life has gone,
The love so passionately sought,
    That was so much your own.

There may be hours when you shall bend
    Beneath a load of care,
When you shall look in vain for one
    Who all your grief would share,
Who would have deemed it happiness
    Life's load for you to bear.

Yet we were happy, and I know
  You loved me for awhile,
You hung upon my lightest word,
  Your heaven was in my smile;
A false, false world set cunning snares
  Your heart from me to wile.

Woe! woe! to those who dig the pits
  For poor unwary feet,
Who make the poisoned cup of sin
  So exquisitely sweet,
Who stay not till their victims fall
  Is certain and complete.

THE LETTER BOX.

YES, cast them in, some fraught with woe,
  Some blistered o'er with hate,
Some bearing burning words of love,
  Some terrible with fate.

Some whispering hope and happiness,
  Some maddening in despair,
Some painting life a blissful scene,
  All stored with pleasures rare.

Some calling it a weary load
  A thing of toil and tears,
Some sick with disappointed hope
  And worn with jealous fears.

Some full of tender, trusting love—
  The heart in every line—
Some from dark clouded lonely lives,
  Who 'neath earth's sorrows pine.

Some writ as tho' the pen were steeped
    In wormwood and in gall,
Raising 'twixt tried and trusty friends
    An adamantine wall.

Some quivering o'er with new-born hope
    All tremulous with bliss,
And bearing on their blotted leaves
    The impress of a kiss.

Some full of anguish and remorse,
    And useless vain regret,
Filling the heart with grief and love—
    And some with sad tears wet.

All bearing into waiting homes
    Or tidings good or ill,
Making hearts leap with rapture high,
    Or stand with horror still.

Yes, cast them in, these messengers
    Of happiness and pain,
Some full of anxious thought and care
    For wanderers o'er the main.

For dwellers in the tented field,
    For rovers on the sea,
Who nightly pray for words of cheer
    From the dear old countrie.

INCORRUPTIBLE TREASURE.

"Behold we count them happy who endure."

SOME treasures moths cannot corrupt,
   Or thieves break through and steal—
A heart of love and charity
   For other's woe to feel,
That the world's teaching cannot change
   Or the world's frost congeal.

A spirit that in every ill
   Thanks God it is no worse,
That e'en in sad affliction's hour
   Can some past good rehearse,
Is better far than rank and power
   And red gold in our purse.

To bear our trials patiently,
   To do what good we can,
To cast our mite in willingly
   To help our fellow man,
To strive, howe'er imperfectly,
   To work out God's good plan.

To feel that many a toiling life
   Has wearier days than ours,
To see the footprints of His love
   E'en in the wayside flowers,
And look for shelter after storm,
   And sunshine after showers.

To eat our crust with thankfulness,
  Nor grudge our neighbour's store,
Nor e'en to better our sad fate
  Our honour's crest to lower,
But trust e'en when the wolf is heard
  To clamour at our door.

To keep our garments white and clean,
  Our soul's thoughts calm and pure,
And learn from the dear patient Christ
  With patience to endure,
Knowing He has us in His care,
  That His word standeth sure.

To cast no stones at other men
  Because their faults appear,
The reckless heart to wrestle with,
  The drooping one to cheer,
To give unto their pain a balm
  And to their griefs a tear.

To breathe the word of gentleness,
  Of pardon and of love,
The cruel wrong to wipe away
  For sake of One above,
Who prayed e'en for His murderers,
  And for their soul's weal strove.

This is to work His holy will,
  This is to praise His name,
This the religion of the heart,
  That putteth pride to shame;
These are the precious things of life,
  Better than wealth or fame.

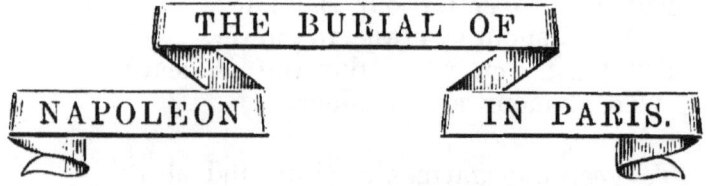

THE BURIAL OF NAPOLEON IN PARIS.

WHERE does this weeping multitude
    So slowly take their way?
What mighty warrior do they bear
    To his long home to-day?

Now, unto me, I pray thee, friend,
    His name and lineage tell?—
Know you not him who wished to lie
    'Mid those he loved so well?

Does there breathe one who has not heard
    The great Napoleon's name?
A time there was when hearts were stirred
    At whisper of his name.

When Europe trembled 'neath his feet,
    And thro' a path of blood
He walked to glory's glittering height,
    And on its summit stood.

When crowns were baubles, kings were slaves,
    And the whole world stood still
To see this master-spirit work
    The dictates of his will.

Oh, friend, I've fought on Jena's field,
    And seen his eagle eye
Light like a torch when he beheld
    The vanquished Prussians fly.

I saw him curb his fiery steed
   On Austerlitz red plain,
And gaze around him pityingly
   Upon the gory slain.

I heard the cry "Vive l'Empereur"
   From lips of wounded men—
Ah! friend, they valued more his smile
   Than crowns or crosses then.

But now they bear him to his grave,
   While o'er the mighty dead
From countless eyes and countless hearts
   The tears of France are shed.

Far, far, upon a barren rock
   He met the tyrant death,
Surrounded by his captors cold,
   He yielded up his breath,

Like some great lion snared at last
   By wily hunters, he
Gave up the soul that could not brook
   Such foul captivity.

Close by the everlasting sea
   They laid him down to sleep,
Far from the hearts that here to-day
   Above his ashes weep.

And evermore the restless sea
   A mournful requiem made
O'er him who slept so quietly
   Beneath the willows' shade,

While wanderers from distant lands
   Would pause upon the sod,
Which covered him who oft upon
   The necks of monarchs trod.

But now is tardy justice done,
  By royal mourners borne,
With kingly pomp they bury him
  To wait the rising morn.

And prayers and tears bedew the path
  By which his body goes,
While white-robed priests their masses sing
  For his great soul's repose.

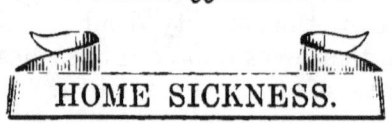

HOME SICKNESS.

WHEN in a foreign land the exile hears
    Some dear, familiar strains of his own land,
Perchance not heard for many weary years,
  How will his head drop down upon his hand.

His manhood for a little laid aside—
  His eyes grow dim with tears at the old strain,
Nor the unwonted weakness does he hide—
  Its tones have led him to his home again.

He feels his mother's kisses on his brow,
  Her gentle words of counsel seems to hear;
Alas, alas! where is that mother now?
  No marvel that he sheds a silent tear.

He hears his brothers' voices and the sound
  Of their blithe feet upon the garden walk,
His sister's arms around his neck are wound,
  He joins once more their laughter and their talk.

That song! 'twas breathed to him in happier days,
  'Tis linked with many a pleasure now no more;
This, this that dims the proud man's eagle gaze,
  And fills his heart with yearnings vain and sore.

There are a thousand memories in that song
   That yet have power to soften and to thrill,
The silent room is peopled by a throng
   Of forms and faces that are cold and still.

Oh, to return—to see the pleasant fields,
   The sparkling waters of his native shore,
With every note a weary longing steals
   To be at home—to be at home once more.

Once more, once more, the dear place of his birth,
   The forms and faces of his youth to see;
Nought seems so fair upon the wide, wide earth
   As thou, *sweet Erin*, where he ne'er may be.

With every note that harp breathed out to him
   The life and beauty of a day gone by,
'Twas this that made his eye so strangely dim,
   And brought, fresh from the heart, that yearning sigh.

TRUE FORTITUDE.

TO bear unmoved misfortune's stroke,
   To struggle bravely on,
To feel the iron entering in,
   And yet to make no moan.

To see in all a Providence,
   To rise even from the dust,
Whate'er your fate, to look above,
   Thro' good and ill to trust.

To see hopes wither, joys depart,
   Yet to be strong the while,
And even in the darkest hour
   To wear a hopeful smile.

Oh, more than Spartan fortitude,
    Grace by religion given
To bear the thousand ills of earth,
    And look thro' all to Heaven.

THE HAUNTED MIND.

After Nathaniel Hawthorne.

IN the depths of every human heart
    There is a silent tomb,
And it open's oft to the watcher's eye
    In the midnight's lonely gloom.

In an hour like this, when blessèd sleep
    The weary eyelid flies,
A funeral train comes round the bed,
    And buried ghosts arise.

Your early love, with mournful smile,
    So sadly pale and fair,
With her garments all faded and defaced,
    And dust on her golden hair.

With echoless steps her form will glide
    Across the chamber floor,
She will look for a moment in your face,
    Then back to her grave once more.

She had loved you well—you turned away
    A fairer face to seek,
Then faded the lustre from her eye,
    The roses from her cheek.

She died, and though never a word was breathed
   You knew her secret well,
And wild remorse and vain regret
   Now in your bosom swell.

Her form flits by, and a sterner one
   Is standing by your bed,
'Tis the demon who first to paths of sin
   Your youthful footsteps led.

See now the writhing lips of scorn,
   The mocking, glittering eye,
Blush, blush, and hide your face, oh, man,
   Your shame is passing by.

Oh, 'tis well, 'tis well for the sleepless one
   If a yet more fearful band
Do not gliding come, with noiseless step,
   Around his bed to stand.

What if remorse should wear the face
   Of the friend of early youth,
Your boyhood's friend—yet you blasted him
   By envy and untruth.

What if the fiend should steal to you
   In a woman's floating dress,
With wild reproach in her burning eyes
   And sin-stained loveliness.

If your injured friend and your murdered love
   Should stand before you now,
With scorn and reproach on *his* pale face
   And a brand upon *her* brow.

If her hair should drip with the horrid sound
   Of water foul and dank,
If you hear her cry in the silent room
   As 'neath the waves she sank.

And if on your silken couch of state
    This ghostly thing should lie,
Would you not turn your face to the wall,
    And pray that you might die?

What! if there enters a horrid form
    In garments of the dead,
With bloody stains on the winding-sheet,
    The blood that you have shed.

Oh, God in his mercy pity those
    To whom such ghosts arise,
Better for them they had ne'er been born—
    Oh, would that men were wise.

Could they see the bitter fruits that spring
    From seeds they madly sow,
Would they not reap some present peace,
    And be spared much future woe?

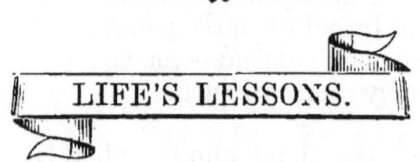

LIFE'S LESSONS.

OH, look not back into the past,
    It can return no more,
God's purposes are deep as vast,
    Your way still lies before,
Onward and hope that at the last
    Your foot may touch Heaven's shore.

Oh, look not back, save to be warned
    By dangers you have known,
The counsels you so oft have scorned
    Now all your care must own,
The robe your idol that adorned
    To fluttering rags has grown.

The flowers that carefully you nurst
  Have withered in your hands,
Your air-blown bubble, long since burst,
  Only your scorn demands ;
And in its nakedness accurst
  Your folly shivering stands.

Improve the present, God has given
  The present for our good,
We prize it not, yet much of Heaven
  It teaches, if we would
But strive to work out the old leaven
  Even from our daily food.

The daily sorrows, daily cares
  That come alike to all,
The thousand pitfalls and the snares,
  The ills nor few nor small,
The bait that the weak soul ensnares,
  The wants that on us call.

These in the present we shall find,
  God's ways are hid in each,
Unlearned, most ignorant, and blind,
  We strive in vain to reach
What unto all our human kind
  God yearns in love to teach.

Yet, fear not, for the weakest heart,
  Resting on him, grows strong,
The future may the good impart
  For which we yearned so long,
And e'en when sinking 'neath death's dart
  We may lift up Heaven's song.

OUR BLIND CHILD.

I SAW, and my heart melted in my breast the while,
  With what a patient, gentle, loving smile
She gave her place upon her father's knee
To her boy brother, because he could see,
Then stood with her long eyelashes cast down
While swept the glittering pageant thro' the town;
And when the thoughtless boy, with eager cry,
Called unto her to look e'er they'd pass by,
I heard the faint, low sigh, and marked the streak
Of vivid crimson on the pure pale cheek;
Yet when I called my darling to my chair,
And said I grieved that she should have no share
In all this gaiety, she swift replied,
"Nay, mother, nay, 'twas not for that I sighed."
Oh, sweet deception, that would hide from me
The deep, deep want, for well I knew that she
Yearned for the day and hungered for the light
Of but one sun on her eternal night.
She is our first-born and our fairest one,
When all the rest unto their sports have gone,
Who glides to the old place—her father's knee—
Or nestles at my side?—ah, who but thee;
Who, when with weary pain my head bends low,
Comes with her little hand as soft as snow
To press it to my brow, while to my eyes
The beauty of thy face is of the skies,
And as I gaze upon its light divine,
I ask myself, with trembling, "Is she mine?"
Who stills her brother's laughter with the word,
Mother is sleeping, but my precious bird,

Who lightens every care, whate'er it be?
Who is my dearest blessing, who, but thee.
One thought oft saddens me—thou ne'er hast gazed
Upon my face, tho' oft thine eyes are raised
When thy dear head reposes on my knee—
Oh, then, my child, I long that thou could'st see,
That thou could'st see the deep, deep love exprest
Which sighs and trembles in thy mother's breast.
In vain my wish—but well I know, my own,
How to thy parents' hearts thy heart has grown,
And tho' thou seest no sun in blue skies blaze,
Nor may on this fair earth a moment gaze,
Nor see thy brothers' faces, dimpling o'er
With joyous laughter on the nursery floor,
And oh, what grieves me most, can mark no sign
Of all thy father's fondness, nor of mine;
Yet oh, not blind, my darling, oh, not blind,
There is a day-spring in thy soul enshrined,
For when at evening prayer I see thee kneel,
I know that God does unto thee reveal
The glories of his Heaven, by the light
That makes it radiant, for so bright
And beauteous its expression, I have felt
A saint and not a child beside me knelt.

——oo——

YES, it is true, and she whom you so prizéd
    Has but deceived you with her whispered words,
The love you lavished forth her heart despiséd,
    And snapt, with careless hand, life's tenderest chords;
Yet, let her go, her love was but a name,
To you be all the praise, to her the shame.

She knew you loved her, and she joyed to see
    The captive bound beneath her chariot wheel—
Oh, how can woman thus deceitful be,
    And wound an honest heart she may not heal;
Woe, woe to those who thus without remorse
Poison life's fountain at the very source.

Oh, it is ever thus—we still are bringing
    Our choicest offerings to be trampled on,
Our richest wealth of love all wildly flinging
    To marble hearts and natures cold as stone,
Worshipping idols that, alas the day!
Melt while we clasp them to their kindred clay.

What castle can we build nor fear the rains!
    What goblet can we drain, nor taste the lees!
We lean on broken reeds, our best sun wanes,
    We look for summer fruits on barren trees;
Our joys are oft ideal, but we know
That mortal man must taste of mortal woe.

Where can we turn to in this changing earth,
    And find no change or shadow in our sky?
Full oft the notes of anguish cross our mirth,
    The opening smile is crushed out by a sigh,
The fondest hope we cling to may depart,
And there's a secret void in every heart.

We trust and hope, and find we were deceivéd
    In those we would have trusted to the last,
O'er unaccomplished dreams we all have grievéd,
    Some cherished thing we to the winds have cast;
The lesson that life teaches us is hard,
And yet the upright soul must have reward.

And better love and lose than never know
    The glory and the beauty love can give,
No fate can from us take the rapturous glow
    It ever leaves us, tho' it did deceive;
There is strange sweetness in the broken string
That once such music to our souls could bring.

And you, who have, alas, too early tasted
    The poison drops of sorrow in life's bowl,
Think not the boon you gave was idly wasted,
    Has it not filled with song your poet soul?
The fount of youth renews itself again,
    And beautiful is sunlight after rain.

For her—may God forgive her—she has planted
    Within a generous bosom many a dart,
And hours must come when conscience, mem'ry haunted,
    Will show her all the work of that true heart,
Once all her own, then haply, richly blest
With the deep fondness of a truer breast.

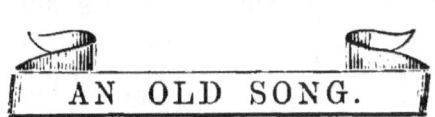

AN OLD SONG.

TELL me why, when I am singing,
    In a plaintive voice and low,
That from hidden sources springing
    Tears unbidden softly flow.

And within his drooping fingers
    Yonder listener veils his face,
'Tis because within him lingers
    Mem'ries time cannot erase.

And so thrilling and so mournful
    Is the sweet old song you sing,
That to eyes tho' seared and scornful
    You have power the tears to bring.

'Tis because you can awaken
    Feelings that have slept for years,
And the pride before unshaken
    Now is humbled into tears.

See the children cease their playing,
   Closer to each other creep,
In their wonder softly saying,
   "Wherefore does the old man weep?"

Ah, they know not he is wringing
   To the vanished past again,
And a voice now hushed is singing
   To his heart that plaintive strain.

As it sang when life was pleasure,
   When his ear with rapture hung
On the old, familiar measure
   You to-night have softly sung.

That is why, when you are singing,
   In a tender voice and low,
That from hidden sources springing
   Tears unbidden gently flow.

―――oo―――

THE WAVES' REPLIES.

ANSWER me, answer me, waves of the sea,
   Say will my lover return to me,
Say will he come with the love of old,
Will his voice be changed or his heart be cold,
Will he bend on me those witching eyes
That first filled my soul with glad surprise,
With the same bright glances that they wore
In those sweet, sweet hours that too soon were o'er,
Ye cruel waves, ye answer me not,
Can the beautiful past be quite forgot?
Oh, I wake in the early morning's light,
And I watch all day till the shades of night,
But in vain, in vain, from sea to sky,
His vessel's sails ne'er meets my eye.

Each morn I rise and keep hoping on
He'll come to me e'er the set of sun,
Each night I lie down with a weight of woe
Such as none but the desolate heart can know.
But what speck is that on the dark blue sea?
'Tis the bark of my lover, 'tis he! 'tis he!
Slow pass the hours till my love I meet,
Beautiful waves, bring him here to my feet;
Forgive me, Heaven, for my doubting heart,
And grant that we never more may part.

―――oo―――

MABEL'S LOVERS.

COME kiss me on the lips, Mabel,
   And kiss me on the brow,
I care not for my cruel doom,
   Death has no terrors now.

For you and Walter Tyrrell
   Have both forgiven my sin,
And I have what I long wanted—
   Heaven's peace my breast within.

Thank God, tho' I am dying,
   My doubts are all removed,
And I know you are the same Mabel
   Whom long ago I loved.

My eyes are opened now, Mabel,
   My eyes are opened now,
The nearer we come to the grave, dear,
   The more clearsighted we grow.

And I see it was all my own folly,
  All my own folly and pride,
Or long ago I'd have made you
  A happy, happy bride.

And 'twas all the jealous doubting
  Of my own rebellious heart,
That has been my curse, my torment,
  And cast our lives apart.

For even if Walter Tyrrell
  Did love you, Mabel dear,
I ought to have known you better,
  And had no selfish fear.

Why did I blame his loving
  What I had learned to adore,
But you know there was more than that, Mabel,
  You know that there was more.

And curséd be the traitor
  Who whispered first to me
That the woman I almost worshipped
  Could false or faithless be.

But I see it all now, darling,
  He loved my Mabel, too,
And his bitter envy made me
  To you and himself untrue.

He told me you smiled on Walter
  While I had been away,
You remember you would not answer
  The question I asked that day.

When I, with my jealous fury,
  Drove the colour from your cheek,
No wonder to one so hateful
  You would not deign to speak.

But that night when I saw you whisp'ring
    With him 'neath the hawthorn tree,
My heart was on fire with rage, Mabel,
    And cruel jealousy.

And I swore a bitter oath, Mabel,
    That I would never stoop
To be first a woman's humble slave,
    And then to be her dupe.

I vowed revenge on the traitor
    Who had stolen my more than life,
God forgive me, I thirsted and panted
    To meet him in bloody strife.

I could not believe then, darling,
    That Walter was my friend,
Oh, deeply I have suffered
    And deeply I have sinned.

I could not believe then, Mabel,
    That 'neath that trysting-tree
He was crushing his own heart's longings,
    And pleading with you for me.

But, thank God, I did not slay him
    On that awful, awful night,
Nay, shrink not away from me, dearest,
    From blood this hand is white.

Come nearer, Walter Tyrrell,
    Come closer to my bed,
And show her the hand she's clasping
    Is not with your blood red.

You have forgiven me, too, Walter,
    Forgiven me long ago,
God bless you, my friend, my brother,
    You bear no hate, I know.

For you came from distant countries
  To comfort my dying bed,
May the blessings God has denied me
  Be showered on your head.

And when I am dead and gone, Walter,
  Mabel will be your wife,
And with her may Heaven grant you
  A long and happy life.

You'll be a better husband
  Than ever I could have been,
Raise my head, Walter, and let it
  Upon her bosom lean.

Mabel, for my sake love him—
  You must make up to him
For the wrong I did—ah, I'm going,
  The light is getting dim.

Has the sun sunk behind the mountains?
  Love, I see not your face,—
Put your arms round my neck, let me hold you
  Once more in a last embrace.

There—now I'm dying happy,
  Kiss me, my own, he said,
Give me your hand, Walter Tyrrell,
  And the restless spirit fled.

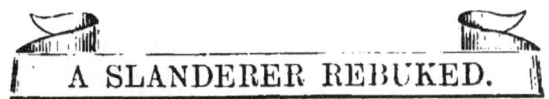

A SLANDERER REBUKED.

BREATHE not that name, unless to praise,
    For tho' 'tis nothing now to me,
In better, brighter, happier days
    How blest was I, how fond was he ;
He was the lover of my youth,
    My heart's first idol, and shall I,
While thou proclaimest a bitter truth,
    Unmoved, unpained, sit calmly by.

If thou hast aught of praise to speak,
    Then of thy voice I cannot tire,
But bring no blush into my cheek,
    And bring into my eyes no fire :
He may be all that thou hast said,
    But wherefore wilt thou wound and wing
The heart that has so often bled,
    And pierce it with another sting.

Oh, thinkest thou I can bear to hear
    Upbraidings harsh and words unkind
Of one who was to me so dear,
    Round whom my heartstrings were entwined ;
No, let the sin be what thou wilt,
    From scorn and censure now forbear,
Thy path, perchance, is free from guilt,
    Because there lurked in it no snare.

No praise to him who walks aright
    Because no other path he's known,
Thy past hath not been all so white
    Hadst thou been left, like him, alone ;
Alone, when blood and pulse beat high,
    A prey unto unnumbered arts,
Too weak to bear, too proud to fly
    The counsels of deceitful hearts.

Say which of us can cast a stone,
  What life is free from shame and sin?
Turn back thine eyes upon thine own,
  And then, oh turn those eyes within;
What seest thou in that hidden place?
  Is it from all pollution free?
If so, thank him who gave thee grace
  To pass unstained thro' life's dark sea.

And show compassion unto those
  Whom the fell siren leads astray,
Ease, if thou canst, their hearts deep woes,
  And for their peace and pardon pray;
Go, o'er their sins and sorrows grieve—
  Go, point them to a pitying Heaven,
Learn like thy Saviour to forgive,
  E'en as thou hop'st to be forgiven.

FREE.

YES, falsest and frailest of women,
  I'm free from your trammels at last,
The meshes you wove are all sundered,
  Your spells to the winds I have cast;
Your beauty no longer distracts me,
  Your false lips no longer betray,
You laid the last burden upon me,
  And, thank Heaven, I flung it away.

No more at the feet of Delilah
  A Samson degraded I kneel,
The withs are all burst that enchained me,
  My strength and my manhood I feel;
Your kiss, I would deem it pollution,
  Your smile, 'tis the lightning of hell,
Your eyes are twin daggers empoisoned,
  That murdered your foe ere he fell.

Go, think of a future fear-haunted,
   Go, think of a past that is red
With the blood of the souls you have blighted,
   And toss on your thorn-bestrewed bed;
Go, bury your shame in oblivion,
   The voice of your conscience go still,
The wrath-cup of painful repentance
   And sad retribution go fill.

THE ESCAPE.

A FRAGMENT.

LORD Ulric feasts within his hall,
   His minstrels strike the tuneful lyre,
A thousand vassals wait his call,
   One only daughter calls him sire.

Hers is the pure, sweet loveliness
   Of opening violet in the spring,
She wears it as her native dress,
   A beauteous, yet unprizéd thing.

To-night a gallant suitor waits
   To win from her one favoring smile,
Great lord is he of fair estates,
   And welcomed by her sire the while.

But she is proud, and coy, and cold,
   And turns her from his suit to sigh
For one who owns not lands nor gold,
   Who may not to her bower draw nigh.

With many a gem and many a flower
   They deck her shining hair to-night,
Her beauty with new charms they dower,
   And praise her dark eyes' tender light.

Now, who will like our lady be,
   At board or dance, they proudly say,
Low drooped her forehead on her knee,
   And turned she from their gaze away.

"Oh, leave me for a little while,"
   She to her bower maidens said,
Her soft cheek brightened with a smile,
   Then coloured to a rosy red.

Then, as their footsteps died away,
   She stripped her jewels from her hair,
And guided by the moon's pale ray,
   Stole swiftly down the castle stair.

Loud sang the minstrels as she past
   The praise of him who sought her hand,
And loudly beat her heart and fast
   As caught her ear her sire's command.

"Now to thy mistress hie in haste,
   Tell her the banquet is begun,
Speed, laggard, speed, the hours we waste,
   To-night is Hilda wooed and won."

She looked up to the silent sky,
   She trembled, but no tear she shed,
Unto the past she gave one sigh,
   Then out into the night she sped.

The snow, the pure, the dazzling snow,
   Veils in its whiteness all the earth,
Hushed is the babbling streamlet's flow,
   And silent is the song-bird's mirth.

How chill, how lone—my father's hall
   Glows with the ruddy logs ablaze,
Ah, even now I hear him call
   Upon my name in wild amaze.

His steed is champing at the gate,
   His sword is girded by his side,
Oh, love, for thee I've braved his hate,
   Oh save, oh shield, oh guard thy bride.

I see his footprints on the earth,
   He's followed by his good greyhound,
Ah, who can bear a father's wrath,
   Woe, woe to us if here we're found.

His glove upon the grass I see,
   And yonder frets his eager steed,
Now, Christ be praised, he comes to me,
   " Oh love, and art thou here, indeed.

" And shall we never, nevermore,
   By cruel hands be torn apart,
Now doubting and despair are o'er,"
   He said, and claspt her to his heart.

" Come let me kiss away the tears
   That hang within thy starry eyes,
Thou hast no cause, sweet love, for fears—
   See the day's king begins to rise.

" And long ere he has sunk to rest
   Within the chambers of the sea,
My dove shall shelter in her nest,
   And who shall take her thence from me.

" My followers are stout and bold,
   My good broadsword is true and tried,
And once within my mountain hold,
   What fate shall harm my bonny bride.

" Aye closer press to mine thy cheek,
   Step proudly now, my gallant grey,
Yes, toss thy mane and arch thy neck,
   Thou bear'st a gentle freight to-day.

"And fail us not, my noble steed,
  We have no hope on earth but thee,
Back, gentles, I the way will lead,
  Let him who loves me follow me."

He said, and in his stirrups rose,
  "Our Ladye shield thee, then," they cried,
"We shall be pathways to thy foes
  Ere they shall harm thy bonny bride.

"Lead on, lead on, we'll do or die,
  'Tis joy to us to work thy will,"
He gazed on them with kindling eye,
  Then turned and led them o'er the hill.

KYLEMORE LAKE.

OH lone Kylemore, oh lone Kylemore,
  The tears will dim mine eye,
While wandering by thy pebbly shore,
  Beneath the silent sky.

Each breeze that wantons o'er thy breast
  Brings airs from purer skies,
And forth upon its useless quest
  My yearning fancy flies.

Each wave that murmurs at my feet
  Doth tell its tale to me,
And mem'ries wild, and sad, and sweet
  Belong, Kylemore, to thee.

They come again, the vanished hours
  Of summer's golden prime,
The song, the sunshine, and the flowers
  Of that delicious time.

Oh, beautiful Kylemore, thy waves
    Are studded o'er and o'er
With hopes that slumber in their graves,
    To live for me no more.

There is strange music in the song
    Thy murmuring water sings,
Yes, dreams of Heaven to thee belong,
    Thou daughter of three kings.

———oo———

TURNING OVER THE LEAVES.

WHAT am I doing all alone, you say?
    Why thinking of old times and scenes,
Of the bright sunny morning of life's cloudy day,
    When I was in my twenties and you were in your teens.

When I was in my twenties, long, long ago,
    And you were budding forth like a rose upon the tree,
My spring of life is past and my pulse is beating slow,
    But the freshness of your beauty my mental eye can see.

Full thirty years have flitted since I looked upon your face,
    And now I see it withered 'neath the chilling touch of time,
But to me it wears the beauty of the old familiar grace,
    'Twas the sunshine of my boyhood, 'twas the mem'ry of my prime.

Ah, many a pleasant day in that bygone time was ours,
    Alas, they flew too quickly, and we counted not their flight,
We have had our golden morning, with its sunshine and its showers,
    Now we're waiting calmly for the coming shades of night.

We have floated in our shallops down the fitful stream of
    time,
  And a single breath may waft us o'er the steep into the
    main,
Let us anchor for a little 'neath the shelter of this lime,
  While we turn o'er the pages of the book of life again.

Here's the first, when merry children on the daisied grass
    we played,
  Wild hunters of the butterfly and chasers of the bee,
When for your golden ringlets a leafy crown we made,
  And filled your lap with roses from my garden's favorite
    tree.

Oh, happy days of childhood, but I turn the pages o'er,
  And a deeper joy is flooding the leaves before me now,
Our way is still together, but as children no more,
  Your voice has tenderer music and a blush is on your brow.

You know that we were lovers in the old days that are gone,
  The days o'er which I ponder in the twilight's lonely gloom,
But you could not give your hand, tho' your gentle heart
    was won,
  And with many tears our youthful hopes we buried in the
    the tomb.

The anguish of our parting, ah, me! I think on still
  The burning words of madness that in bitterness I said
When you told me all was over, for you dared not cross
    their will,
  And I wished we were together in the churchyard cold
    and dead.

But you soothed me into calmness, and I parted from you
    there
  With a holier love and deeper, than e'er I felt before;
See, the page is stained and blotted, once so stainless and
    so fair,
  Tell me not my tears were idle, for my brightest dream
    was o'er.

You wedded one who loved you—a happier fate than mine,
　The woman that I wedded never cared to smile on me,
But to her dreary portion she had learned her to resign
　When the pitying angel called her, and set her spirit free.

There were children at your table, and love beside your hearth,
　And I blessed the God who granted such blessings to your life,
But oh, it grieved me sadly in my spirit's gloom and dearth,
　That tho' I called you angel, another called you wife.

Last night I saw your daughter—she has her mother's eyes—
　Dear child, my whole heart blessed her as she knelt beside my chair,
And she sang a sweet old song till my breast was filled with sighs,
　For 'twas one you used to sing me when the gold was on your hair.

She told me that you loved it, for that many a time and oft
　You would sing it in the twilight till your eyes were dimmed with tears,
Then she added in a whisper, oh so reverent and so soft,
　'Twas prized because 'twas taught you by one loved in early years.

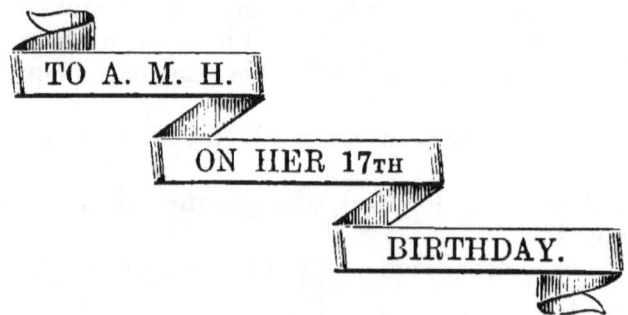

TO A. M. H. ON HER 17TH BIRTHDAY.

CAN'ST thou not hear my spirit's voiceless cries ?
   Canst thou not feel how much I yearn o'er thee ?
Bound unto me by earth's most precious ties,
   In whose sweet face such beauty dwells for me,
Half child, half sister, sharer in the best
And purest dreams that animate this breast.

Gentle enthusiast, in thy pensive soul
   What burning thoughts, what tender fancies lie,
Would that my hand might trace thy fortune's scroll
   With lines as stainless as thy young heart's sigh,
And that from life to death, from youth to age,
No bitter tear should blot the shining page.

Thine is the clinging nature that could love
   With wild abandonment and all believe,
Nought could the anchor of thy faith remove ;
   And if o'er broken trust thy breast should grieve
Yet would'st thou kneel before an empty shrine,
And round thy shattered idols flow'rets twine.

When late I gazed upon thy quiet face,
   Hushed in the beauty of a still repose,
When late I clasped thee close in fond embrace,
   And kissed upon thy cheek the deepening rose,
God knows how earnestly my full heart prayed
Life's cross on thee might tenderly be laid.

TO A. M. H. ON HER 17TH BIRTHDAY.

And as I prayed, methought a golden light
    Filled all the chamber, and beside the bed
Stood there an angel, who, with fingers bright,
    Laid a fair garland on thy sleeping head,
The primrose and the violet both were there,
Hiding their blossoms in thy dusky hair.

I held my breath, and reverently gazed
    On the sweet, solemn face that o'er thee hung,
" Fear not," he softly said, " nor be amazed,
    I am the guardian of the pure and young,
They hear my voice, they touch my clasping hand,
While their souls wander in enchanted land.

" And I am ever near them—God has sent
    Me from the glorious Heavens, my native home,
To watch o'er flowers like this, which are but lent
    To beautify your earth with their soft bloom
Until the day when He shall gather them
By angel fingers home to grace His diadem."

With that a stream of tenderest music stole
    Into the room, and his bright wings unfolding,
This purest guardian of a pure young soul
    Rose and departed from my rapt beholding,
But much it comforts me to know that he
Even in sleep, my child, keeps watch o'er thee.

"ALL FOR LOVE, OR, THE WORLD WELL LOST."

PRESS thy cheek to my cheek,
    Lay thy soft hand in mine,
While thou art beside me
    Dost think I repine.

What are wealth, fame, or fortune,
    Or kindred to me,
When weighed in the balance,
    My own love, with thee?

Would I give up the feeling
    That thou art my own
For the pomp or the power
    Of a conqueror's throne?

Would I barter thy kiss
    For the best gift of fate?
It can give me nought better
    Than thou my soul's mate.

It brimmed o'er my cup
    When it gave me thy love,
And now to the whole world
    I fling down the glove.

With thy smile for my guerdon,
    Thy prayers for my shield,
My steps will not falter,
    My sword shall not yield.

And if I am vanquished
    My comfort will be
That the life thou wilt mourn for
    Was given for thee.

SIR PHILIP SIDNEY.

WHO has not heard of gallant Sidney bleeding
    Upon the gory plain at close of day,
Sore, sore athirst, a cup of water needing,
    Yet, pointing to a soldier, hear him say—

"Give him to drink, his need is more than mine,"
    And so gave up the ghost without a groan ;
Oh, thou, the noblest of a noble line,
    A deathless fame for thee the deed has won.

Of all the names that glow on glory's page
    None wears a brighter lustre in our eyes,
Who in death's pangs another's could assuage,
    And give to a poor hind the needed prize.

Thou wert a second Bayard, gentlest, best—
    "A lamb at home, a lion in the field ;"
A woman's heart beat 'neath thy steel-clad breast,
    Strong to defend the right, the weak to shield.

Would there were more like thee, more who could bear
    To see the cup pass by them, nor complain,
Who in life's battle would the water share,
    And give to those athirst, nor ask again.

INVOCATION TO THE MUSE.

COME, my Muse, nor linger so,
    Fold thy wings beside me,
All my love, thou well dost know,
    Tho' I sometimes chide thee.

Thou hast been my constant friend
    When all else departed,
Giv'n me pleasure without end
    E'en when heavy hearted.

When I hungered thou hast fed,
    When I languished blessed me,
Twined a garland for my head,
    And with smiles caressed me.

When in solitude I wept,
    None I pined for near me,
Ah, how often hast thou stept
    To my side to cheer me.

Brutish natures, dull as lead,
    Cannot see thy beauty,
Cannot hear thy gliding tread,
    Love with them is duty.

I have laughed unto myself
    When they dared to flout thee,
They, forsooth, in pride of pelf,
    Can do well without thee.

Richer far am I with thee
    Than their gold possessing,
For new charms each day I see
    In thee, my best blessing.

INVOCATION TO THE MUSE.

Riches may take wings and fly,
   Gross enjoyments perish,
But, my Muse, both you and I
   Nobler pleasures cherish.

Let the dull fool hug his store,
   When my hearth thou sharest
I have piles of golden ore
   And of gems the rarest.

He has stores of precious things
   Which have been denied me,
But I sup with queens and kings
   When thou art beside me.

Poets, princes, heroes come,
   All their glories showing,
'Till o'erflows my humble home,
   My heart, too, o'erflowing.

Lovely ladies, queens of old,
   Maidens fair and holy,
Some in robes of cloth of gold,
   Some with presence lowly.

All with beauty on each brow
   Thou could'st give them only,
Come, my Muse, and bless me now,
   Come, for I am lonely.

Haste, sweet goddess, why so slow,
   Fold thy wings beside me,
All my love thou well dost know,
   Tho' I sometimes chide thee.

TO —— ON R —— WEEPING.

I HAVE seen the wealth of a virgin heart
    Laid down on pity's shrine,
I have seen the blood to a pure cheek start
    At a grief and wrong of thine,
And tears on that cheek, rare, priceless gems
    From feeling's golden mine.

Oh, blest be the grief that has bidden such tears
    From purest sources flow,
And blest be the wound where such balm is poured,
    For now, indeed, I know
There are angels lingering still on earth
    White as unsullied snow.

In my soul there was rev'rence sweet and strange
    As I watched those falling tears,
Methought I had past o'er a weary waste
    Of sinful, stormy years,
And I felt like one who, with holy joy,
    The gate of Heaven nears.

Oh, child, may the Mighty One have heard
    Thy spirit's voiceless prayer,
And when a crown of unfading light
    Thy spotless brow shall wear,
May those you have loved in the world of woe
    Your bliss eternal share.

A CONNEMARA GIRL.

MY fair-haired forest girl, my mountain maid,
    Oft wilt my heart recal thy winning wiles.
Thy glances, sunshine laden, given unweighed,
    Unmeasured, and the wealth of smiles
That lingered ever round thy roseate mouth,
Where dwell the perfumed odours of the south.

Within the dimples of thy downy cheek
    The loves and graces evermore abide,
And when thy violet eyes mine own will seek
    Methinks twin fairies in their blue deeps hide,
Mischievous sprites of frolic and of fun,
But when thou weepest, child, my heart's undone.

For as the flower which to the sun's fierce blaze
    Its fairest petals shrinketh to display,
But joyous turns to meet the dew always,
    And gives to night what ne'er it granted day,
Thy grief more than thy gladness thee endears,
More dewy bright thine eyes when seen thro' tears.

Bright, happy tears which from the fountain spring
    Of pure, deep feeling, " such as angels shed,"
Eileen mavourneen, may those angels fling
    Soft, thornless roses on the path thou'lt tread,
And oh, may Heaven never, never let
With bitter, bitter tears thy cheek be wet.

And now, my pale, white flower, adieu, adieu,
    My water lily with the golden leaves,
Thy mountain home is fading from my view,
    But o'er its woods and wilds my spirit grieves;
My path leads o'er the hills—a time-worn track—
But to the past my heart looks fondly back.

And shall look back for ever to those days
  When loving fingers round my own would twine,
And dear eyes flash forth welcome—in the dusty ways
  Of life hereafter I will not repine—
But those sweet, kindly faces will recal,
  And pray that in their "lives, no rain may fall."

———oo———

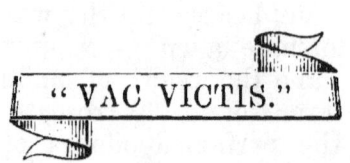

"VAE VICTIS."

I WOULD I were in that blest place
  Where all this toil would cease,
Where, gazing on my Saviour's face,
  I might have endless peace,
Where, lying on his loving breast,
I might have recompense and rest.

There never more a cruel word
  My tortured soul might wring,
My heart by foulest wrong be stirred,
  Or writhe beneath venom's sting,
No pain or shame would curse me there,
No hidden stab, no carping care.

Marked from the first by some dread blight,
  My life has ever been
A long, long never-ending night,
  A shifting, chequered scene,
A useless struggle with my fate,
Which must be dark and desolate.

A landscape—where a fitful sun
  A chilly radiance shed,
A battle lost as soon as won,
  Where hearts have inly bled
And died—tho' not a single stain
Crimsoned the surface of the plain.

"VAE VICTIS."

I have been worshipped, and my cheek
   Has glowed 'neath passion's kiss,
Hush, treacherous heart, why wilt thou speak
   In such an hour as this;
With the dead past thou'rt long since done,
The dull, drear present is thine own.

With love and hope I've nought to do,
   My dreams are laid aside,
The goal has faded from my view,
   Mine is an ebbing tide,
One wave which all my fortunes bore
Returns not to life's dreary shore.

Oh, God! the pangs of fruitless love,
   The loss of murdered hope,
The strong must still successful prove
   When might with right doth cope,
Woe to the vanquished—woe and doom—
A galling chain—or bloody tomb.

Mine is the chain, and, oh, its weight
   Hangs heavy on my heart,
And when the wrong is sore and great
   Some haunting thing will start
Out of the past, until I cry
"Let me forget it, God, or die."

A WOMAN OF FASHION.

'I MUST have a box at the opera, dear,
   Says charming Lady Grace,
And I think I must get Madame Rachel soon
   To enamel my pretty face.

Late hours and dancing are trying, indeed,
   But what can a woman do?
And for so little she'll wonders work,
   Give you beauty fresh and new.'

My carriage is getting quite out of date,
   I saw such a lovely thing
Standing at Storr and Mortimer's, dear—
   You must get me one this spring-

Harry can wait for a year, I'm sure,
   He's too young to be sent to school—
Oh, I have not shown you my last new dress,
   With the sweetest trimmings in tulle.

Lord Alfred told me at Lady C's
   I looked lovelier every night,
But I will not wear that moiré again,
   It makes me a perfect fright.

Pray don't look sulky, I'm sure I spend
   But a very small sum in dress,
Indeed, if I am to go out at all
   I cannot do it on less.

Stay in to-night and chat with you?
   Dear—how romantic you've grown—
What would they say if they knew that you
   And I played Darby and Joan?

You wish I could spare my children some time,
    What are you fussing about?
Do you think I can go to the nursery now,
    Just as I'm drest to go out?

Nurse has been telling you tales, I see,
    Something the matter with Bell,
I'm sure when I saw the children last week
    They both looked healthy and well.

I can't disappoint Lady C, you know,
    I promised to be at *her* ball,
Can't you go sit at your club, my dear,
    Or give some old friend a call.

Or if you don't like going out to-night,
    There's the new novel to read,
Now, Charles, I'm sure it is very hard,
    You are very unkind, indeed.

Looking as if I had said something wrong,
    And I'm certain I heard you swear,
There, Pauline, I think I am ready now,
    Put this diamond in my hair.

Has the carriage come round, 'tis striking twelve,
    Are the children not yet in bed?
Charles, will you ring, I'm sure I hear
    Some footsteps overhead?

There, never mind, 'tis some nonsense of Bell's,
    Don't I look well, Pauline?
Yes, I think Lord Alfred will surely say
    That I am beauty's queen.

Your master has gone, well, I never met
    Such a bear in all my life,
Heigho, if I was as wise as I'm now
    I'd never have been his wife.

Be sure and sit up for me—give me my fan—
  I think I'll be home by four,
Quick, button this glove—yes, come at last,
  The carriage is at the door."

The rosy hands of the coming dawn
  Were drawing night's sable veil,
When the lady entered her stately home,
  Her cheek as her roses pale.

While one with a brow of anguish stood
  To wait her coming there,
His face had grown old in a single night
  With agony and despair.

" Well, Charles, you see I am early to-night,
  But you look like a ghost," she said;
" Madam, you come back an hour too late,
  Your little girl is dead."

―――*oo*―――

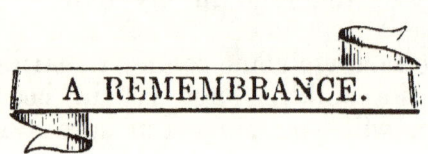

A REMEMBRANCE.

I REMEMBER how she loved me
  In the old days that are gone,
I remember how she trembled
  At my lightest whispered tone.

How her dear eyes used to brighten,
  And her soft cheek used to glow,
When her hand clasped mine in meeting
  In the sweet hours long ago.

A REMEMBRANCE.

I have gazed on other faces,
   I have looked in other eyes,
I have seen the flush of feeling
   To fairer cheeks arise.

But a love so pure and perfect
   I never more may meet,
May God my madness pardon,
   I crushed it 'neath my feet.

In soul and mind a woman,
   A child in trust and love,
So lofty and so tender,
   And pure as saint above.

She feared not for the future,
   She doubted not the truth
Of the idol of her girlhood,
   Whose kiss to her was ruth.

Oh, God! the hand she trusted,
   The hand which once caressed,
Was that which drove the arrow
   Deep in her gentle breast.

Lost love, thy toil is over,
   The anguish and the strife,
And the love is with thee now in death,
   Which spurned thine in life.

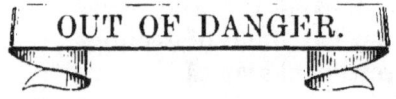

OUT OF DANGER.

WE welcome thee back from the shadowy land
    Where thy feet have wandered long,
And our praise is given to the gracious hand
    Which changed our sighs to song ;
We wrestled with him, and he gave us thee,
And we humbly thank him on bended knee.

We welcome thee back, we welcome thee back,
    Thou art all our own once more,
We writhe not now on doubt's awful rack,
    The shadow has left our door.
The cloud is lifted from off our home,
Thou wert all too bright for the ghastly tomb.

We stand and dream, tho' with unshut eyes,
    Oh, God ! if the words were spoken,
If, spite of our groans, our anguished cries,
    The golden bowl was broken ;
Then, bereaved of thee, we were bereft,
But, Jesu be praised, thou still art left.

Oh, love, we have missed thee from thy place,
    We have missed thee everywhere,
We have looked in vain for thy winsome face,
    For the gleam of thy golden hair,
We have listened oft for thy bounding feet,
For thy gladsome voice and thy laughter sweet.

Oh child, we have stood by thy couch of pain
    With breaking, bursting hearts,
While our tears fell fast as summer rain ;
    Ah, me, when hope departs.
And fear, in its chilly grave clothes drest,
Creeps silently into each aching breast.

How cold and chill is the fireside hearth,
 How dark the sunniest noon,
Yes, God's precious gifts were of little worth
 Were we still denied this boon;
Thy life, beloved one, thy life He gave,
And, oh, not in vain did our sick souls crave.

He bowed himself from His glorious throne
 To hearken to our distress,
Ah, gentle Saviour, in ages gone
 'Twas ever Thy joy to bless,
There was one who besought Thee, with bitter crying,
For his little daughter who lay a-dying.

And now, as then, Thou did'st o'er her bend
 To whisper "Maid, arise,"
Dear, never-changing, eternal friend,
 In Thy home beyond the skies,
Thou did'st pity us as Thou pitied him,
And drove from our darling the tyrant grim.

Yes, we hold her, we clasp her, we fondly gaze
 On the face we love so well,
The veil from the awful past we raise,
 And our grateful bosoms swell
With thanks to that Saviour who heard our crying
For our little daughter who lay a-dying.

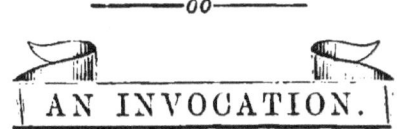

AN INVOCATION.

STRETCH out thine arms to me, and come thou near,
 Bridge with thy mighty love the heaving wave,
Hast thou long sought for me?—then I am here,
 And thou wilt comfort me, will bless, will save;
I have been, oh, so weary—but at last,
At last the bitterness of life has past.

AN INVOCATION.

Say wilt thou love me less because the tears
   That have bedewed my cheek had poisoned springs,
I hear thy gentle chiding of my fears,
   As to thy honest heart my heart close clings;
Yes, let me lean upon thy gen'rous breast,
Hast thou not given to me of gifts the best.

Oh, there is recompense for bygone pain,
   Oh, there is rest for weary, wayworn feet,
And as the thirsty flower drinks up the rain
   When, drooping low, it lies 'neath summer heat,
So do I drink the draught poured out by thee,
And drinking, know it will be well with me.

I close my eyes, and let a blessèd peace
   Steal to my soul—I had not dreamed that ever
This aching craving at my heart would cease,
   I thank thee, God, who art the gracious giver,
Did'st thou not send this life to search out mine,
To teach me the great deeps of love divine.

Lord, thou art full of pity, wounding only
   Where thou can'st pour the balm to soothe and heal,
Oh, my soul's friend and lover, I was lonely,
   And now it is so sweet to know and feel
I shall not sit in darkness any more,
For, lo, a sunbeam stealeth thro' the door.

The glitt'ring thing makes all the chamber bright.
   I'll lay down my head in the golden track,
How beautiful it is, how warm, how bright;
   What saith the Scripture—" They shall never lack
Any good thing who put their trust in Me,"
I trust my God and bend a rev'rent knee.

THE POST BAG.

OPEN the Post Bag—what comes here?
"My sweetest love, my dearest dear,"
And all the rest just like to this,
With fifty vows and many a kiss,
And all to end in sighs and frowns,
A life-long curse, or lawyers' gowns.
And what comes now?—from some dear friend—
"Sir, if you don't by next post send
That ten pound five, so long now due,
I'll bid my attorney write to you;"
But can't my readers guess the rest,
Oh, may such writers all be—blessed.
Now humble pie—"Most honoured sir,"
(This to some petty, worthless cur,
Who, just because you chance to be
Placed in his power, will let you see
That he is master, quite forgetting
That your sun may rise when his is setting,
And that some time you'll have your day;
However, we have nought to say
To those who are so much our betters,
Let us return and read their letters).
"Most honoured sir," but, on my word,
I can't the humble pie record,
'Tis "if you please," and "be so good,"
And much that stirs rebellious blood,
Till, for my part, I'd rather grant
Ten thousand favors than one, want.
Now comes what thrills and melts the heart,
In this no meanness has a part,
But words of kindliness are here
That waken an unwonted tear,
And makes us feel we're not bereft

Of all earth's good while this is left,
Here's news which came o'er land and seas
That brings us humbly to our knees
In thanks to Him who shielded those
How dear to us He only knows,
And here's some record of a faith
That triumphed in the hour of death,
And we are told our friend has past
Away to his reward at last,
And that he died as brave men die,
With childlike trust and courage high.
The letters lie—a motley crew—
White, black, and yellow, green and blue;
Some a faint odorous perfume bear,
That shows the touch of lady fair,
It makes us think the hand was white
And soft that did the words indite,
Could we but break that tiny seal
What histories might the page reveal,
But we'll not seek to know e'en part
Of that strange compound—woman's heart.
Here is a rough and misspelt thing,
Shall we aside impatient fling
The soiled and blotted envelope ?
No, it is rich with many a hope,
And warm with many a fervent blessing,
Tender as mother's fond caressing,
Mary and Pat have hearts as well
As Frederick and Isabel,
And love is here perhaps more true
Than in the scented billet-doux.
Tis a strange jumble—love and hate,
From humble poor and wealthy great,
The creamlaid and the crested note
Sail with coarse foolscap in one boat,
It doth remind me of that spot
Where all distinctions are forget,
And young and old, and rich and poor,
Pass in together by one door.

"BY THE HOPE WITHIN ME SPRINGING."

"By the hope within me springing,"
   By the light thy love has shed,
By the fond thoughts to thee winging,
   Scattering blessings on thy head,
     By the renewal of my youth,
     By thy tenderness and truth.

Think of me when daylight stealing
   From the chambers of the East
Cloudy glory is revealing
   In that world so bright and blest,
     Where the hills of Heaven rise
     From the mystery of the skies.

Think of me when dews are falling
   On the leaves of waiting flowers,
Hear my spirit to thee calling
   In the lonely midnight hours;
     See my shadowy form and face,
     Clasp me in thy soul's embrace.

Breathe thy soul in tender sighing
   As I lean upon thy breast,
Hear my heart in fond replying,
   Let its meaning be exprest
     In the pulsing of its blood,
     Bounding in tumultuous flood.

A CHILD'S QUESTIONS.

CHILD, to your childish questions,
    Asked with eager lip and eyes,
My heart from out of its prison
    All earnestly replies,
Yes, there is a world, my darling,
    Far above those clear, calm skies.

It is true—you cannot see it—
    No matter, child, 'tis there;
Its walls are of pearl and jasper,
    Ah, love, when I despair
God sends me thoughts of the city
    Where all is bright and fair.

You wonder why I keep thinking
    Of that far-off, unseen place,
And I see a tender pity
    In your sweet, uplifted face,
While vainly amid the cloud-world
    You strive my world to trace.

Fair is your home, my Bertha,
    Stately its walls and towers,
And blithely beneath its shelter
    You are passing life's happiest hours,
Oh, that I might for ever, darling,
    Keep the serpent from the flowers.

Alas, in the Book 'tis written
    That so it may not be,
There will come a day, my Bertha,
    When my world you will see,
When you, too, learn the lesson
    Long since learned by me.

A CHILD'S QUESTIONS.

When you know, as, alas, I know it,
　　How dark this earth appears
To those who gaze on its beauty
　　Thro' a mist of blinding tears,
To those who in vain are hungering
　　For the joys of other years.

I am old, and worn, and weary
　　Tho' my hair is not yet grey,
If you were tired, my darling,
　　With your childish toil or play,
Would you not like on my bosom
　　Your little head to lay.

Yes, I know how you would nestle
　　Your soft, fair cheek to mine,
Then when your chamber was flooded
　　With the holy, pale moonshine
I would lay you down on your pillow
　　In slumber to recline.

So, I have grown tired, my Bertha,
　　Tired of earth's care and pain,
The pillow for me is waiting
　　Where all my fathers have lain,
And when I have slept a little
　　I will waken up again.

I will wake in the lovely city
　　That is far above those skies,
Wake no more a weary woman,
　　With tear-beclouded eyes,
But wrapt in a robe of glory
　　From that long sleep I'll rise.

I know that I speak in riddles,
　　You cannot yet understand
How near, yet how far, is the beauty
　　Of that mysterious land
To which we are journeying daily,
　　Led by God's mighty hand.

But I know that hand will teach you,
   I know that hand will guide,
I must leave you one day, my darling,
   I must steal out from your side,
But He will be with you ever,
   In Him you will abide.

And whene'er in your childish bosom
   A thought of me will rise,
Then remember beyond the mountains
   A glorious city lies,
Beyond the blue of those mountains,
   And above the blue of those skies.

And in that glorious city
   Still waiting shall I be,
Till, 'mid thy sister angels,
   Thy sweet face I shall see,
And hear thy soft voice blending
   With Heaven's minstrelsy.

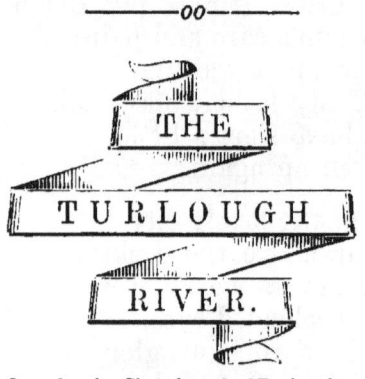

THE TURLOUGH RIVER.

The Turlough River flows by the Churchyard of Turlough—quite under its walls.

THE woods, the fields, the verdant hill,
   The village church, I see them still,
     Of Turloughmore;
The sloping lawn, the ruined tower,
As last they looked at evening's hour
     In days of yore.

The stately home that once was mine,
Whose casements in the moonbeams shine,
    The gateway old ;
The bridge, with battlements and pier,
Thro' which the river, calm and clear,
    To ocean rolled.

Oh, river rushing to the sea,
How often have I paused by thee
    In dreamings fond,
Striving, with questioning face and pale,
To raise the future's misty veil,
    And look beyond.

How oft with scented bud and flower,
Gathered in many a wild-wood bower,
    I've strewed thy waves ;
And watched them on thy bosom glide,
Borne on by the resistless tide
    Down to their graves.

Thou did'st a lesson to me teach
If I could read thy voiceless speech,
    Oh, current free ;
So down the stream of hurrying life
We rush, with hope and purpose rife,
    To death's dark sea.

So onward thro' the world we go,
On to the end, be it swift or slow,
    Till o'er the steep,
With one long sigh, one shuddering breath,
Into the gulf that yawns beneath
    We wildly leap.

But such were not my childish dreams,
I only saw thy rippling gleams
    Thro' banks of green ;
I only heard thy tuneful song
While thou did'st swiftly sweep along
    Thro' the fair scene.

Into thy waves the sweet woodbine,
The wild rose and the eglantine,
   Their perfume shed;
And round about thy margin grew
The primrose pale and violet blue,
   In leafy bed.

So into my young life was poured
Of fancy's flowers a magic hoard,
   Earth, air, and sky
Were teeming with the beauty bright,
The visions of a young delight,
   Born but to die.

Oh, river gliding to the sea,
Thou bear'st a pensive memory
   Of bygone years,
That calls from out their silent sleep
Dead hopes and dreams, and ope's the deep
   Of secret tears.

Dear friends, whom I shall see no more,
Whose feet have touched the silent shore,
   Have trod thy brink;
Have gazed upon thy dimpled breast
With smiling faces, hearts at rest,
   Oh, let me think.

Oh, let me think, let me retrace
My way through the familiar place,
   Let me live o'er
The love, the confidence, the truth,
The days of my departed youth
   In Turloughmore.

Come back ye lost, ye loved return,
Recross the shadowy, silent bourne
   For one short hour;
Here is the mossy, rock-piled seat,
Twined round and round with wild briar sweet
   And passion flower.

Here is the spot where oft we stood
To gaze upon the dark pine wood,
    Its boughs ablaze
In the departing monarch's smile,
Just pausing on his march awhile
    For one last gaze.

Here at the close of peaceful day
We listened to the song-bird's lay,
    Hand clasped in hand;
Here watched we the bright stars appear
Above us in the ether clear,
    A glittering band.

And the pure radiance of that sky,
The glory that came flitting by
    On wings of night,
But thrilled us with a deeper sense
Of rapture exquisite—intense—
    And new delight.

Oh, river rushing to the sea,
No voice I call may answer me,
    No sound I hear,
Save the unceasing, rapid flow
Of thy wild song, now sweet and low,
    Now loud and clear.

No flowers I scatter on thee now,
But many a broken, blasted bough
    Of hope's fair tree,
And many a dream and purpose high,
And many a quivering, long-drawn sigh
    I give to thee,

Oh, river rushing to the sea,
I kneel in solitude by thee.
    And sad tears pour
Into thy waters, gliding down
By verdant mead and forest brown,
    Thro' Turloughmore.

I kneel and kiss the waving sedge
That flutters on thy winding edge,
    I kiss the stones
Once trodden by the feet that never
Shall wander by thee, gentle river,
    That hear'st my moans.

Oh, when the dark, dark gulf is past,
And on the Heavenly shore at last,
    All pain is o'er,
I would my body they should lay
To moulder till the Judgment Day
    In Turloughmore.

There in the quiet summer eves,
Amid the hush of whispering leaves,
    My dust might hear,
Like some familiar, well-known tread,
Thy solemn requiem o'er the dead
    That slumber near.

———oo———

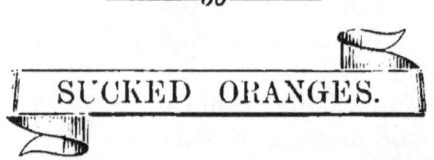

SUCKED ORANGES.

SUCK your orange, then throw it away,
  "Tis a lesson taught us every day,
Work a brute till he fails on the road,
Strive to rouse him with spur and goad,
Curse him as lazy, forget the past,
And leave him to die in a ditch at last.

Welcome your friend while his hope is new,
If fortune smiles will not you smile, too?
But if in misfortune his head he would hide
Why pass him by on the other side?
Like the worn-out hunter, he had his day,
And an orange sucked must be thrown away.

Fondle the woman whose love you won,
Smile and caress till the web is spun,
But when thorns bestrew her path
Visit on her your righteous wrath,
What can she in her madness say
But an orange sucked must be thrown away.

Lover seek not your lady's bower
While shadows over your pathways lour,
If with her you would still find grace
Seek her ever with smiling face,
Learn that the motto of lady gay
Is suck your orange, then throw it away.

Cheated lover and slighted friend,
If your best hope fail you in the end
'Tis but the story often told,
The world's heart is hard and cold,
And this lesson is taught you every day—
That an orange sucked must be thrown away.

———oo———

CHURCH OF ST. NICHOLAS, GALWAY.

CALMLY beneath those tombstones
  Slumber the sacred dead,
The soft light of the evening
  Gleams on each lowly bed,
Without the restless ocean
  Its mournful requiem sings,
And to mine ear it speaketh
  A world of solemn things.

Here lie the young and lovely,
  The good and kind lie here,
Oft are these loved names watered
  By many a bitter tear,

For many a dream and longing
  Lie these low graves beneath,
And many a high aspiring
  Is ended here by death.

Here slumbers one whose summons
  Came in the bloom of life,
Not weary of the struggle,
  Not tired in the strife,
Cut off without a warning
  While yet his sun was high,
And men stood still to marvel
  How one so blest could die.

Oh, deep the voiceless anguish
  That broods this grave above,
This mute, this sad memento,
  This shrine of buried love;
Weep as thou wilt, pale mourner,
  Thy tears fall idly here,
The reaper old but whetteth
  His scythe with every tear.

Here sleeps a weary pilgrim,
  Worn with the toilsome fight.
Worn with the tears and tossings
  Of many a day and night;
Sick of the fleeting pleasures,
  Sick of the dreary waste,
Sick of the Dead Sea apples,
  So bitter to the taste.

Sick of the fitful sunshine,
  The faint light in the gloom,
Longing for calm and quiet,
  And rest within the tomb;
Worn with the ceaseless striving,
  The seeking after rest,
And now the clods are lying
  Unmoved upon his breast.

Here, deaf to tears and crying,
    The loved and lovely sleep,
Unmoved by the sad mourners
    Who o'er them vigils keep;
And such shall be my pillow,
    And such shall be my bed,
The grass upon my bosom,
    The carved stone at my head.

And such shall be my dwelling
    When all earth's show is past,
Here to this solemn company
    I, too, shall come at last;
After "life's fitful fever"
    This shall be my abode,
To ripen till the morning
    When men shall meet their God.

To ripen till the morning
    When gleams the great white throne,
Then shall the dust be gathered,
    And bone cleave to His bone;
Oh, blessèd dead now sleeping
    My dear Lord Christ in thee,
Oh, Death! the gate to glory,
    Thou hast no fears for me.

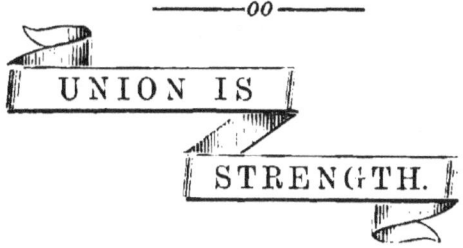

UNION IS STRENGTH.

L AND of Russell and of Sydney, land where Hampden bled and died,
Land of Milton and of Shakespeare, land of freedom and of pride,
Hear my voice, which calleth to thee far across the moaning tide.

Land of statesmen and of poets, land of heroes and of kings,
Land, whose very name an ægis o'er her freeborn children flings,
'Tis to thee, oh, glorious country, I would strike my wild harp's strings.

I am not an alien, Albion, I am of thy soil and blood,
What, tho' wide between our mountains rolls the everlasting flood,
The same stream that feeds my being warms thy great heart true and good.

When thy bravest led the legions of our armies in the fight
Did not my whole soul go with thee and my sons in harness dight
Rose like giants at thy bidding to uphold thee in the right.

Strike together, men and brethren, for the altar and the hearth,
Ask not is it Albion, Erin, or old Scotia gave you birth,
Children of one mighty mother, zealous for her weal and worth.

Boundless be your peace and plenty and your glory endless be,
Higher than the clouds above you, deeper than the circling sea,
Which, for ever foaming round us, holds us scathless, proud, and free.

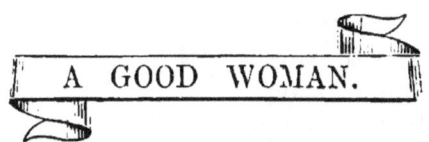

A GOOD WOMAN.

A companion picture to a poem by Owen Meredith.

A WOMAN should be pure and fair,
   Her mission every woe to share,
     Her joy to love;
And to be loved with faith sincere,
Deeming this gift of gifts most dear
     'Neath Heaven above.

Her heart with tend'rest pity filled
Like odorous scents from flowers distilled
     Her life should be;
A yearning all things to forgive,
While in her gentle breast should live
     Sweet charity.

Sweet charity for other's sin,
Sweet hope that all may Heaven win;
     A holy faith
And trust in rest beyond the sky,
And patience that will glorify
     A bed of death.

A fortitude in trial's hour
O'er which no tempter can have power,
     Her only law
Her sense of right; and tho' by pain
And suff'ering seared, yet free from stain
     Or marring flaw.

Her world should be her sheltered home,
Nor from it should she care to roam
     To giddy scene;
Her empire here, her sweet domain,
Where she in gentleness doth reign
     By love a queen.

Mistress of every winning grace,
Her eyes the sunshine of the place;
   Her tender song
And her light foot upon the floor
The music that our souls adore,
   Nor deem it wrong.

A ready wit to catch and see
The airiest shaft of raillery;
   A soul to feel,
To sympathise, to share, admire,
And to all noble things inspire;
   A tact to heal

Where others may inflict a wound;
When such a woman we have found
   We know that God
Has to our lives an angel given
To lead us on the path to Heaven—
   A glorious road.

THE MUSE'S DEFENCE ON HEARING HER CONTEMNED.

WHO'S he that scoffeth at the Muse,
   And calls her worship madness?
May wicked sprites him now misuse,
   And turn his mirth to sadness.

His eyes, unused to tender tears,
   Looks in her sweet face boldly,
He knows not of her hopes or fears,
   But tramples down both coldly.

He never felt the bliss of love,
   Or yet the pain of pining,
On to his kindred clods he'll move,
   His life's great business—dining.

Who's he, because his purse is full,
   Looks down with scorn upon her,
And thinks, dull fool, and poor as dull,
   She deemed his notice honour.

Was not his vision blinded so
   By earth's gross mists and vapour,
And that his soul's lamp ever low,
   Has dwindled to a taper.

Before the scorning on her brow
   He'd shrink away in terror,
But she, at chiding ever slow,
   Forbears to mark his error.

Who's he, because his birth is high,
   Thinks that he bends to greet her—
She had her birthplace in the sky,
   Where angels joy to meet her.

She stooped from her high throne awhile
   To bless us by her smiling,
We feel the sunshine of that smile
   E'en half our cares beguiling.

Who's he that comes with lagging foot
   And measured words and phrases
To proffer to the Muse his suit
   And stammer out his praises.

He comes because his brethren come,
   And knows not why they're kneeling
But half with mute amazement dumb,
   He feigns what they are feeling.

Binds the scales closer on his eyes,
  And leave him still pursuing
His narrow round—she doth despise
  Such forced and tardy wooing.

She must be wooed, as women are,
  With tenderness and ardour,
For lukewarm love a suit will mar,
  And make its winning harder.

But when the lowliest lover kneels
  With truth to pour his passion,
Her tender soul his fondness feels,
  And pays him in like fashion.

Oh, Muse, oh blessing of our life,
  Thou sunshine never fading,
Thou calm in midst of vexing strife,
  Thou joy in man's upbraiding.

I clasp thy yielding hands in mine,
  I kiss thy lips and tresses,
I pour thee out my soul's best wine,
  My heart thy footprints blesses.

Let those who have no power to feel
  In ignorance despise thee,
We, we, who love thee round thee kneel,
  It is the fool that flies thee.

THE DEVIL'S HOLIDAY.

HIGH on a mountain crag the Devil sate,
    And gazing on the scene with devilish pleasure,
Bade his surrounding satellites not bate
    Their fiendish efforts, but fill up the measure
Of the doomed city's woe, then laughing, cried,
" Now is my hunger almost satisfied

" Down with it to the ground, hark to its moans,
    How warmly flows along that bloody tide,
How pleasant to mine ear its shrieks and groans,
    Here, here at least my name is deified ;
Hence, minions, to your work, away, away,
This is your master's feast, your monarch's holiday."

Then forth upon their tasks the hellish crew
    Went gleefully, in their foul hands
The signals of destruction, as they flew
    A groan uprose that spread o'er seas and lands,
Men's curses, women's wailing, and the cry
Of feeble age and slaughtered infancy.

And now a roar like thunder rent the sky,
    And 'neath death's sable banner wide unfurled
In blackened ruins on the red earth lie
    The wonders and the glory of a world,
While from afar the Devil smiled to see
The horrid din, the awful revelry.

There brother slew his brother, son his sire,
    Infant and wife and mother, hoary priest
And shrieking maiden, while a rain of fire
    Reddened the summer sky from west to east,

And, as the work of woe went madly on,
Shook every dome from roof to basement stone.

All Europe heard and trembled, and a cry
  Of mingled anger and of sorrow rose
From every nation, when, the smoke pass'd by,
  Men saw fair Paris writhe in mortal throes,
Her beauty laid in ashes, all defiled,
The mother murdered by her sucking child.

Oh, crown and pride of France, thy people's joy,
  How is thy glory gone, thy garments stainéd,
Crushed as a child might crush its gilded toy—
  For thee the world's heart is sorely painéd;
No time or art can unto thee restore
The grandeur and the glories that are o'er.

Thy sacred things profaned by ruthless hands,
  Thy hero's image trampled in the mire,
While round it grouped the sanguinary bands
  Who glutted here in vain their savage ire;
Did they not tremble as thy calm face fell,
Nor fear his shade who loved their land so well.

Oh, desolated city, by the tears thou'st shed,
  By this dread cup of wrath and fiery pain,
By shattered palace and by heaped up dead,
  By every blighed heart and ruined fane,
I bid thee rise and let thy sons go free
From the accurséd thrall of infamy.

Rise from thy ruin, France, and give no more
  The devil cause for laughter, he has had
A fearful harvest, bid his joy be o'er,
  Nor at thy blood and tears let him be glad;
Fair, lovely land, would thou could'st feel and know
How the world weeps with thee thy shame and woe.

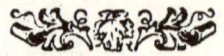

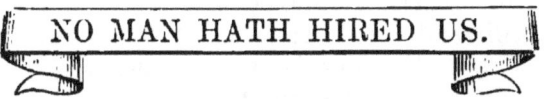

NO MAN HATH HIRED US.

"Why stand ye here all the day idle, and they said, because no man hath hired us."

NO man hath hired us, we have watched and waited,
    Waited with patience thro' the live long day,
To some dread doom our hopes seem ever fated,
    And now, at evening's close, we sadly say—
        No man hath hired us.

No man hath hired us, we are strong and willing,
    Our hands are iron, and our nerves are steel,
Our hearts with noblest impulses are thrilling,
    Yet all in vain, these strivings must we feel—
        No man hath hired us.

No man hath hired us, many feet go by us,
    Speeding with joyful haste the road along,
They care not for our state, they come not nigh us,
    Unnoticed and unknown we bear life's wrong—
        No man hath hired us.

No man hath hired us, we have aspirations,
    We have quick bosoms, chafing at delay
What is our life—a chain of enforced patience,
    Till our warm pulses cool, our heads grow grey—
        No man hath hired us.

No man hath hired us, oh, ye hearts nigh broken
    'Neath the dread burden that the poor must bear,
Not in unheeding ears the words are spoken,
    One mightier than your fellows knows your care,
        He will have pity.

No man hath hired us, know you not, oh, mourners,
"They also serve their God who stand and wait ;'
Many of this sad creed are haughty scorners,
   Yet not alone the mighty who are great,
      The great are patient.

Not now, not here, but in the grand " for ever,"
   Shall the strange riddle of our life be read,
Sorrow from earth, alas, we may not sever,
   But in the Heavenly vineyard none have said,
      No man hath hired us.

———oo———

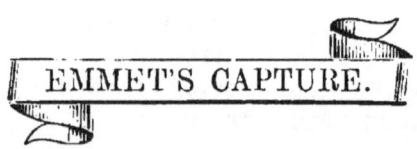

It is well known that Emmet was seized in Curran's garden, while saying farewell to Sarah Curran, to whom he was betrothed.

"ARISE, awake, e'er the day doth break,
   I have crossed o'er mountain and moor,
Passed thro' flood and fire and dangers dire
   To stand without thy door.

"The bloodhounds fleet have tracked my feet,
   A price is on my head,
But I'd rather die than from thee fly
   With my last farewell unsaid.

"Arise, awake, ere the day doth break,
   For I dare not linger here,
Let me clasp thy neck, let me kiss thy cheek,
   Let me breathe my last sigh in thine ear.

" Let me bear o'er the sea dear thoughts of thee
    To sweeten my lonely lot,
Ere I go away let me hear thee say
    I shall never be forgot.

" By this pledge I've worn I will soon return
    To bear thee o'er the wave,
Or I will lie 'neath a foreign sky,
    In a nameless, lonely grave."

She hath ope'd the door, she hath flown once more
    To the breast she loved so well,
He has clasped her neck, he has kissed her cheek
    Whereon both their sad tears fell.

Oh, the pain, the bliss of that parting kiss
    Sure none but lovers know,
And the strength of the love that rose above
    Their anguish and their woe.

With footsteps slow he has turned to go,
    But, alas, he was bought and sold,
One hand is laid on the shrinking maid
    And one on her lover bold.

Her frenzied cry rings wild to the sky,
    One groan speaks his despair,
Then helpless he stands 'neath their arméd hands,
    As the bird in the fowler's snare.

As the hounds the deer, they have tracked him here,
    And here he now must yield,
They plucked from his side the sword once dyed
    With the best blood of the field.

Then she stilled her moan, but cold as the stone
    Was the hand in his she laid,
And closer she prest to his faithful breast
    As their last farewell was said.

"Farewell, farewell, this is my death-knell,
    I ne'er shall behold thee more,
This kiss is our last, all, all is past,
    Our bright, brief dream is o'er.

"For the felon's doom and the prison's gloom
    Are what await me now,
Woe to thee and me, yet to God's decree
    We both must learn to bow.

"To thee and to Heaven my life is given
    Oh, land that I could not save,
Love, mourn not so, or I cannot go
    With firmness to my grave."

"Go, noblest and best, to thy glorious rest,
    They shall not us long divide,
For me will be room in thy narrow home,
    And in death I'll be thy bride.

"Thou hast graven thy name on the roll of fame
    In letters that cannot fade,
From the bloody dust of the brave and just
    Are future heroes made.

"They may strike thee to death, but the victor's wreath
    Unwithered shall deck thy brow,
And weep not for me, I have lived but for thee,
    And thy love is my comfort now."

He went to his death with unquickened breath,
    She faded with the flowers,
But their pain now o'er, they have met once more
    In a fairer world than ours.

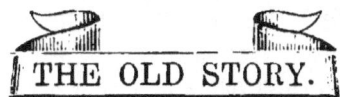

THE OLD STORY.

YOU say I'm sadly altered, Ned,
    Within the last few years,
I've learned the truth of woman's kiss,
    The worth of woman's tears.

'Tis strange that such a byegone pain
    Has power to hurt me yet,
Old friend, at times I've almost prayed
    To curse her and forget,

Sit here beside the hearth, dear Ned.
    And I will tell you all,
Just let the firelight on your face
    It's flickering radiance fall.

You say I'm sadly changed and worn,
    I did not know till now
That tho' the wound was deep within
    It's marks were on my brow.

I've struggled hard thro' everything
    To bear a manly part,
But wherefore need I hide it now—
    She well nigh broke my heart.

I kept a brave front to the world,
    I was not one to whine,
I tried to think it was God's will,
    And never would repine.

But, oh, at night, I oft have sobbed
    And moaned out like a child
For the sweet face that long ago
    Into my own has smiled.

Not e'en to you, my comrade true,
    Could I the old wounds bare,
But I have seen her dead to-day,
    No more the mask I'll wear.

I'll tell you all, for one moon more
    Will see me on the wave,
I'll wait until the grass is green
    Upon her quiet grave.

I'll wait until the grass is green,
    And then I'm off to sea,
East or West, or North or South,
    'Tis all alike to me.

'Tis the old thing—her foolish heart
    Believed a traitor's tale;
Our wedding day was near at hand—
    The fire that makes me pale.

There, give me time, I'm better now—
    One eve I went to meet
Her in our own old trysting-place,
    I listened for her feet.

I listened for her joyous voice,
    I hungered for her kiss;
Oh, God, it makes me mad e'en now
    To think or talk of this.

They came together through the wood,
    Her head was on his breast,
His false, false lip was prest to hers,
    His hand her hair caressed.

I cursed them with a mighty curse,
    And from the spot I fled,
Then never, never saw her more
    Till now I saw her dead.

When morning dawned they sought for her—
　　Poor wanderer, never more
The treshold of her happy home
　　Her erring feet crost o'er.

Her father fretted for his child,
　　Her mother pined away,
She was their all of joy on earth—
　　They died upon one day.

And I, I laid them in the grave,
　　Where soon I'll lay her, too;
Ah, Ned, before the awful last
　　My face and voice she knew.

I found her dying at my door,
　　My love, my lamb, my pride;
Oh, would that in your happy youth
　　You in my arms had died.

I bore her in and laid her down,
　　Poor lost one, on my bed,
So worn, so wan, so ghastly white,
　　She seemed already dead.

I chafed her famished hands in mine
　　Until her senses came,
And then her poor, pale, wasted cheek
　　Blushed crimson with her shame.

And, with a moan, she dashed her head.
　　My, darling, 'gainst the wall,
But I, thank God, I kissed her lips,
　　Kissed and forgave her all.

I drew her back upon my heart,
　　I bade her shelter there,
And from her brow put softly back
　　Her tossed and tangled hair.

The hair with which in happier hours
    My fingers loved to play—
Nay, do not chide me for these tears,
    I'm not a man to-day.

She looked at me—her yearning eyes
    Will haunt me till I die,
"Forgive, forgive," she faltered out,
    I kissed her for reply.

Then a strange glory lit her face—
    Ah, now that all is past—
I know she came back to her troth,
    She loved me at the last.

For wild she claspt her wasted hands,
    And as her spirit fled
I heard my name with blessings breathed,
    And then she fell back dead.

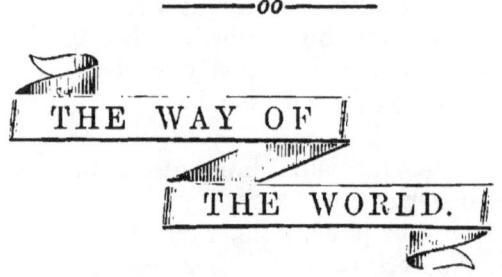

THE WAY OF THE WORLD.

THE way of the world's to spend your life
    In serving a thankless lord,
To find too late 'twas on barren ground
    Your choicest gifts were poured.

The way of the world's to break the hearts
    Of those who are good and true,
To slight old friends if they're down the hill,
    And to flatter and fawn on new.

THE WAY OF THE WORLD.

To pass by a man on the other side
    If his coat is getting old,
To kneel at the shrine of the idol self,
    And to worship the Moloch—gold.

Knowledge was power in days of yore,
    Money is power now,
It can draw in its train the mightiest man,
    Make the haughtiest lordling bow.

The way of the world's to smile in your face,
    * "And murder you with that smile,"
To rejoice when it leads the innocent
    Into ways of sin and guile.

To charm the eye of the thoughless one
    By many a pleasant lure,
To spread a net for unwary feet,
    To grind the helpless poor.

To cringe and whine at a rich man's door,
    To hunt a poor one down,
To greet the one with a bending head,
    The other with chilling frown.

To bid the tired starveling work,
    The desperate outcast pray
While hunger is gnawing at the heart
    That curses the light of day.

To stretch no hand to a sinking man,
    But push him beneath the wave;
To hurry the broken-hearted wretch
    To the shelter of the grave.

---

* "And I can smile and murder while I smile."—RICHARD III.

The way of the world's to labour and toil
    For that which is not bread,
To mock at the fable—constancy—
    And without loving, wed.

To veil 'neath the hand the bitter tear,
    To check the rising sigh,
To bear with calmness a deadly stroke,
    Then hide the wound and die.

To mask the sting that unkindness gives,
    To fight a glorious fight,
To struggle with want as an "armed man"
    And misfortune's cruel blight.

To be beaten to earth a thousand times
    A conqueror at last to rise,
To meet disappointment at every step
    And sorrow in every guise.

To wait and hope, and to live to see
    Both waiting and hoping vain;
To grow faint with the weary march of life
    And sick with the sad heart's pain.

Oh, strange and bitter the world's ways,
    A mournful tale at best;
But, ah, there's a land where no tears are shed,
    And where the weary rest.

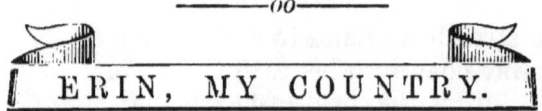

ERIN, MY COUNTRY.

OH Erin, my country, the home of the Graces,
    The birthplace of fairies, and witches, and fays;
The land of warm hearts and of soul-speaking faces,
    Thou'rt dear to thy sons as in palmier days,
        Erin acushla, Erin aroon.

Oh Erin, my country, thy green hills of beauty,
  Thy fields and thy valleys smile fair as of old,
In the grand march of nations do thou but thy duty,
  And thy peace shall be boundless, thy glory untold,
    Erin acushla, Erin aroon.

Let the great trust the humble, the humble give gladly
  That honour and love that are better than wealth,
And no more may the wail of the orphan rise sadly,
  Or the hand of the murderer slaughter by stealth,
    Erin acushla, Erin aroon.

Let the strong use with justice the power God gave him,
  Nor turn a deaf ear to the cry of the poor,
No more let the worship of Mammon enslave him,
  The hope of the needy be his to ensure,
    Erin acushla, Erin aroon.

Dear land of my birth, oh, fain, fain would I bring thee
  All joy and all blessing, all comfort and peace,
With a glow at my heart, oh, my country, I sing thee,
  And that heart shall still love thee till being shall cease,
    Erin acushla, Erin aroon.

Fair darling of nature, thy praise has been sounded
  In language that burns by thy children gone by,
What eye has not sparkled, what pulse has not bounded,
  As thy bards waked the music that never shall die,
    Erin acushla, Erin aroon.

'Neath the green turf that nursed them for ever lie sleeping
  Those great ones, those loved ones who gloried in thee,
By the urns of thy dead a sad watch thou art keeping,
  Yet thou know'st not oh land, what hereafter may be,
    Erin acushla, Erin aroon.

Dear land of my love, this scant wreath that I bring thee,
  Not worthy thy brow, I lay low at thy feet,
With a glow at my heart, oh, my country, I sing thee,
  And would wish that for thee my poor song were more meet
    Erin acushla, Erin aroon.

REMORSE.

OH, look not so, for I can bear
   Aught save thine anguish, thy despair;
Curse and upbraid me, if thou wilt,
Add shame to shame, heap guilt on guilt,
But, oh, I cannot bear to see
Thy sorrow and thine agony;
It maddens me to think that I,
Who for thy sake would gladly die,
Have wounded in its tenderest part
Thy loving, faithful, noble heart,
Have blighted in its sunniest hour
The beauty of thy life's sweet flower;
Yet, oh, by all thy hopes of Heaven,
Say that in time I'll be forgiven.
I do not ask the blessing now,
While thou art smarting from this blow,
But when away long years have fled,
And I am numbered with the dead,
Then, if thou can'st, forgive this wrong
While on thy soul past memories throng
Of times and scenes ere yet my name
Was seared by sin and stained by shame;
When I was like thee pure and good,
Ere evil passion fired my blood—
Sinless and happy, not as now,
With writhing breast and aching brow.
Farewell—oh, never more thou'lt be
Condemned to look on wretch like me,
Accursed as Cain, I'll cross the wave,
To find in other lands a grave;
The past, the future, reels my brain,
I dare not think on these again—
The past, so beautiful and bright,
The future, cheerless as the night
When not one star in Heaven appears.

What! dost thou weep—are these thy tears?
Thou pitiest me—oh, say, oh, speak,
Is it for me they dew thy cheek,
For me and my most wretched fate?
Thou wilt not curse me, then, nor hate;
Wilt pity, pardon—oh, my love,
My broken-hearted, wounded dove,
God in his mercy ever bless thee—
Nay, nay, I do not dare caress thee,
But let me low beside thee kneel,
Thy pity pierces me like steel,
Thy tears are drops of liquid fire—
What! dost thou raise me, higher yet higher,
Are these thy kisses on my face?
Am I, indeed, in thy embrace?
Now I am strong, I will not shrink,
The cup with firmness I shall drink;
Yet while I clasp thee must we sever,
Farewell, farewell, farewell for ever,
The dream, the blessèd dream is o'er,
Thou'st pardoned me—I ask no more.

———oo———

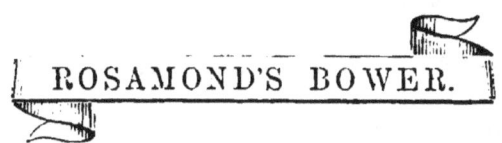

ROSAMOND'S BOWER.

THE birds were singing merrily and perfume filled the air,
When deep within old Woodstock's bower sat Rosamond the fair,
And all in brilliant day-dreams lost, bright dreams of happy love,
She watched to see her lover's form come to her thro' the grove.

She waited, with her longing eyes fixed on the path he'd come,
Waited with wildly-throbbing heart, unconscious of her doom—
Unconscious that the fatal shaft e'en now had towards her sped,
Or that the bolt suspended hung 'bove her devoted head.

Ah, Rosamond, unto thine arms no lover comes to-day,
Never will Henry's fingers more with thy bright ringlets play,
Never again will thy soft eyes gaze on his well loved face,
Never again wilt thou be claspt within his fond embrace.

Instead of kisses, thou must taste to-day the poisoned bowl,
Instead of whispers, bitter words must stab thy tortured soul,
Instead of England's monarch, comes the dark and grizzly King,
And for thy sweet, delicious dream a fearful reckoning.

Why comes he not, she musing said, his usual hour is past?
Hark, what was that, I cannot tell, my poor heart beats so fast,
A footstep—'tis my lord, my love—swift to the door she flew,
But, ah, what stranger form is this which sternly meet her view?

A woman with revengeful eyes, and proud imperious mien.
Great Heaven, it bursts upon her now, before her stands the Queen,
Her dreaded rival—ah, poor Rose, prepare, thine end is near;
Say wherefore lingers Henry now—would God that he were here.

For in her hand she holds a bowl—alas, poor Rose, for
  thee,
Yet, love, false love, thou wert the cause of all this
  misery;
Oh, why in this sad world of ours will heart still seek for
  heart
When might and right stand stern between to cast them
  far apart.

No pity—nought but furious hate—in Eleanor she sees,
And stretching out her snowy arms, she sinks upon her
  knees,
"Oh, spare my life for Henry's sake, spare me," she wildly
  cries,
Roused by the name to more than rage, the vengeful
  Queen replies—

"Drink of this cup, or, by my soul, I'll stab you where
  you kneel,
False minion, you shall now the hate of Eleanor feel;
Ay, call upon your absent love—he'll answer you, I trow,
When he has set his spear in rest and laid aside his bow."

"Is there no pity? Oh, my love, if thou wert here to-day
This cruel Queen would not have dared, thy Rosamond to
  slay;
Lady, he loved but me, but me, I pledge him now in this
With lips yet fragrant from the touch of his last parting
  kiss."

She took the cup, she drank the wine—her soul is going
  fast,
One longing look upon the scene of all her bliss she cast,
Then with a prayer for Henry's weal she, softly closed her
  eyes,
And at her rival's feet ere long a lovely corpse she lies.

And still the pensive traveller will pause upon his way
To gaze upon the grassy mound where murdered Rosa lay,

The spot where, like a nymph of old, amid her flowers she
  dwelt,
While low beside her on the earth her royal Henry knelt.

Then musing on the happy time ere yet the haughty dame
With poisoned bowl and dagger keen to Woodstock's bower
  came,
He'll sigh that in this world of ours heart still will seek
  out heart
When might and right stand stern between to cast them
  far apart.

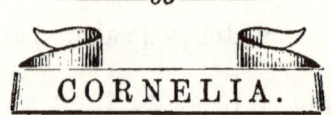

CORNELIA.

THESE are my jewels—dost thou think
    That I could envy thine?
In thy rich casket can one gem
    Compare at all with mine?

Are not my children's eyes more bright
    Than any diamond there?
What pearl or ruby like to these,
    Tho' rich they be and rare?

Oh, dost thou think I envy thee
    Thy chains of glittering gold,
While I can call these babes my own
    Is not my wealth untold?

There is more gold in one bright tress
    Of this soft, clustering hair
Than in the rich and costly things
    That thou hast gathered there.

Go, sit beside thy childless hearth,
    Thy brow with bright gems deck,
Put bracelets on thine arms of snow,
    And chains around thy neck.

But hear no voice and see no face
  That thou can'st call thine own,
And feel with all thy gold and gems
  That thou art still alone.

Then see me with my bright, brave boys
  Kneeling around my knee,
And think that one so blest as I
  Could never envy thee.

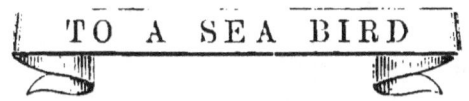

TO A SEA BIRD

SEEN MANY MILES INLAND.

BIRD of the snowy wing and mournful cry,
  I hail thee as a friend, but thou should'st be
Where waves lift up their heads as mountains high—
  Back to thine home, this is no place for thee;
Yet stay with me a little, I would fain
Ope memory's prison gate, loose fancy's rein.

Thou dost restore again what ne'er may be,
  Thou dost recal me joys that live no more,
I breathe my native air, so pure and free,
  I hear in my soul's ear the breakers roar;
I'm at home again in that lone isle
Round which the very ocean seemed to smile.

Oh, mountains grand and hoar from which I caught
  My love for all things lovely—waters wild
And breezes pure, whose every breath was fraught
  With dreams poetic for the island child;
I am your worshipper as in those days
When first my rude harp hymned its song of praise.

Ye were my earliest friends, and fain would I
    Unto your gentle company return,
But sooner shall unclose the death-sealed eye,
    Or life be kindled in the funeral urn
As the quick pulse and throbbing heart be mine
Which make us feel that we are half divine.

Oh sea, oh shore, oh happy childish days,
    Oh, dreams as golden as the clouds at eve
When the departing sun his richest rays
    Flings o'er a world he seems as loth to leave;
I trace my name upon your soft white sand,
I kneel to catch your billows in my hand.

Too faithful memory, how plainly now
    I see the shell-strewn beach, the gleaming towers,
The old, old house, with chambers quaint and low,
    In which were nurst my childhood's earliest hours;
The porch, with western window, where I'd run
To catch the last glimpse of the setting sun.

The fields where oft in infancy I played,
    The fairy dells, with buds and blossoms bright,
The little osier bower my brothers made,
    The blazing hearth round which we grouped at night,
While from some chosen volume one would read,
And back to glories gone our spirits lead.

Oh, hospitable roof, which never yet
    Refused its shelter to the old or poor,
And fireside gay, round which were often met
    Blithe, cheerful faces in the days of yore;
Grey is thy master's head and old to-day,
While weary is the heart that then was gay.

There ever welcome waited on the guest
    Whom fortune wafted to our lonely shore,
There kindly hands on him their favors prest,
    And soothed and cheered him till the storm was o'er;
Then bade God speed him as he launched again
To seek his distant home beyond the main.

TO A SEA BIRD.

Come with me now and climb the ruined fort,
   And gaze down on the waves that seethe below,
Proudly it stood the guardian of our port,
   While in its buttressed walls a goodly show
Of loopholes tells us that in days gone by
Here war and slaughter did their red trade ply.

We'll stand and watch the white-sailed fishing boats
   After their daily toil to anchor glide,
Hark to the challenge hoarse from lusty throats,
   Mellowed to softness by the swelling tide,
Now home each wends his way, and the profound,
Calm beauty of the night is shed around.

Here is the corner 'neath the broken wall
   In which, with tender care, my flowers were set,
This nook once held the volume, worn and small,
   Still sweeter to me than my mignonette,
Those tender songs o'er which I used to brood
Till I grew faint from the delicious food.

How beautiful the landscape, through the fields
   Of waving corn how soft the breezes blow;
Let us return—o'er all my senses steals
   A flood of happy feeling—well I know
This path, smooth trodden by the bounding feet
That never on life's road again may meet.

Oh, dear dead faces that no more, no more
   In fond affection may be prest to mine,
Ye take your peaceful rest—your warfare o'er,
   And for these blessèd ones shall we repine?
No; they have fought the fight, and now the vast
Eternity is their's—life's sorrow past.

Dear, quiet home, where peace and plenty reigned,
   What fell fate drove us from your happy walls?
For what returns no more my heart is pained
   And for its household gods my sick soul calls
Come back—but in the stillness far-off waves
Seem moaning o'er dead joys and grass grown graves.

I dreamed and wake—vacant is now the hearth
　Where children gathered round a mother's knee,
While snatches of old song and bursts of mirth
　Bubbled from hearts as full of careless glee
As now their full of sadness and pale fear,
Which then they never deemed could come them near.

Mine island home, farewell—I owe to thee
　These halting rhymes—therefore I dedicate
To thee my song. The eternal soul is free,
　And though I often chafe at the curst fate
Which prisons me in cares nor few nor light,
My soul's lamp burneth ever purely bright.

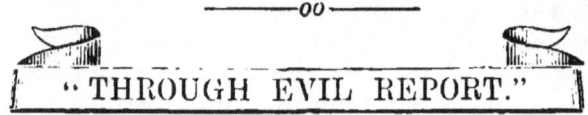

"THROUGH EVIL REPORT."

THOU art left to me still, my bonnie, bonnie love,
　Then why should I despair;
If thou'rt left to me my bonnie, bonnie love,
　For the world's frown I'll not care.

Let it work its worst, my bonnie, bonnie love,
　It cannot alter thee;
And nothing can harm me, my bonnie, bonnie love,
　As long as thou'rt left to me.

As I walked thro' our town on yesterday morn
　One passed me by with a sneer,
And another gave me a welcome cold,
　But did I heed them, my dear.

No, I looked on their faces, poor crawling worms,
　I lifted my own up high,
And I felt there was one, my bonnie, bonnie love,
　Who would never pass me by.

But a month ago, my bonnie, bonnie love,
　They would kneel to kiss my feet;
'Tis the way of the world, my bonnie, bonnie love,
　But little I heed them, sweet.

Oh, little I heed them, the cowards cold,
  Frown or smile is alike to me,
For thou'rt left to me, my bonnie, bonnie love,
  And my world is made up in thee.

FAIRY LAND.

IT is my fairy land—no foot profane
  May ever enter on my soul's domain ;
One chamber in my heart, one secret bower,
In which I wander in the twilight hour
Will only open when the clue I give,
'Tis there I love and hate and breathe and live ;
There shapes of beauty hover o'er my head,
Aerial visitants of "fancy bred,"
With waving tresses and with snowy wings—
Softly they speak to me of wondrous things.
In tender, tuneful voices, and each tone
Is only heard by me—by me alone.
They tell of where unfading flow'rets grow,
Of wand'ring rivers that, with rippling flow,
Steal thro' the blossomed beds of rich perfume
That never droop or change their golden bloom ;
There, on each bending spray, the woods among
The wild-bird pours untired her thrilling song.
And happy lovers wander hand in hand
O'er the green turf of that enchanted land.
And none are weary there or heavy-hearted,
And none who love are ever, ever parted ;
No sighs are breathed, no bitter taunts e'er spoken,
No kiss unvalued and no troth-plight's broken,
No graves are there, no mourners, and no tears—
What sound is that my eager fancy hears ?
Is it some seraph's song—some angel's tread—
" Why, bless my soul, the girl's not yet in bed !"

FLEETING.

THE hand you touch so lightly now
   How often you have prest,
With words of passion, sweet and low,
   To your warm lips and breast.

The face on which you coldly look
   Once haunted you in dreams,
You saw it in each babbling brook
   On which the pale moon beams.

The voice whose accents now you hear
   With an unquickened breath
Once had the power, it was so dear,
   To loose the grasp of death.

Another's voice enchains you now,
   Another's hand you hold,
Before another's shrine you bow,
   To her your vows are told.

And I—I, also, hear unmoved
   The voice so dear before;
Say can it be that we have loved,
   And that we love no more.

If our's was love, it passed away
   As passes morning's dream,
It was the passion of a day,
   A bubble on life's stream.

A truer breast I lean upon,
   A fairer face you found,
Thank Heaven, we both have long since won
   Balm for our bosom's wound.

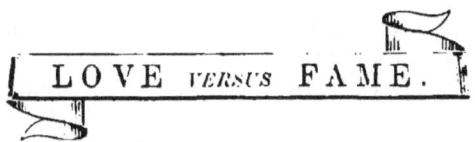

LOVE *versus* FAME.

WHEN my eyes wander over history's page
    My heart leaps up as at a trumpet blast,
I melt with pity, or I glow with rage,
    While hanging o'er the annals of the past.

I glory in the deeds that men have done—
    They were not men, but gods, in those old days;
When at great Marathon the field was won
    I give the Athenians few, their meed of praise.

In the dread pass " three hundred" I behold,
    Their perfumed locks loose floating on the air,
Each warrior cast in more than hero's mould,
    Each sworn to conquer or to moulder there.

I see upon the bridge that spanned the flood
    The brave Horatius take his noble stand,
And when on Roman earth he safely stood
    I stretch my hand thro' time to grasp his hand.

But wherefore need I look to Greece or Rome
    For deeds of valour done by valiant man,
I turn from far my wandering vision home,
    And my heart burns within my breast again.

I stand with mighty Edward on the hill
    " Where Cressy's battle fatally was struck,"
I feel my eyes grow dim, my pulses thrill,
    While 'neath the tramp of steeds the red plain shook.

I see bold Harry drawing in his train
    The captured monarchs of the Bourbon line,
I see the shattered ships of baffled Spain,
    While from afar the good Queen's banners shine.

I hear within my ears the brave words ring,
    As gleams the light upon her burnished helm—
"And think (foul scorn) that any Prince or King
    Shall dare invade the borders of my realm."

Before my watching eyes a noble band
    Of mighty warriors, deathless heroes, pass,
The wonder and the glory of our land,
    They rise before me now in memory's glass.

For them there is no dying—"for to live
    In hearts you leave behind is not to die;"
I muse and wonder till I almost grieve
    I had not being in the days gone by.

And yet the story of Leander dying
    For his young love has more of charms for me;
I hear from her high tower sad Hero's crying,
    I see him sinking in the billowy sea.

I mourn with her, poor captive at the gate,
    Longing and listening for one loving word;
He was her all, her life, her hope, her fate,
    She, only, his "beloved in the Lord."

I weep with hapless Juliet in the tomb
    Beside the pale form of her deathlike lover;
I sigh o'er their sad fate, their young lives doom,
    And with a wreath of flowers their graves I cover.

Beautiful ghosts, you flit along my path,
    I hold your ashes in a fancied urn,
More beauty unto me your sad fate hath
    Than dwells in that which bids my cheek to burn.

PEACEFUL EVENINGS.

DEAR peaceful evenings, can I e'er forget you,
    Dear quiet room, the very shrine of home,
In some safe corner of my heart I'll set you,
    To be remembered in the days to come.

The warmth, the light, the comfort of the place,
    The calm that filled me as I entered it,
But, more than this, than all, the kindly face
    That would on either side the ingle sit.

The friendly hands stretched forth in welcome warm,
    The words so simply kind, yet so sincere;
Oh, heart that's tossed about in life's rude storm,
    Would peace be yours, I bid you enter here.

Here the most vexèd soul must calmer grow,
    Here noble thoughts are nurst and nourished,
Here poesy's sweet stream doth softly flow,
    And blest religion moves with holy tread.

Here simple pleasures, simple joys are found,
    Here counsels wise and good are gently given;
I feel as tho' I tread on hallowed ground,
    Or wandering, press awhile the path to Heaven.

Oh, chamber quaint and old, when far away
    I take my journey o'er life's trackless sea,
Oft shall I hear again the good man pray
    His nightly prayer on humbly bended knee.

His holy head, with silver fitly crowned,
    Will rise from out the past—a beacon blest;
Dear reverend head, much comfort have I found
    While gazing on thee, much of soothing rest.

And when tormented by earth's fret and care,
　Perchance in future hours I fail or faint,
Oh, may the seed thou'st sown good harvest bear,
　And hope and memory hush the vain complaint.

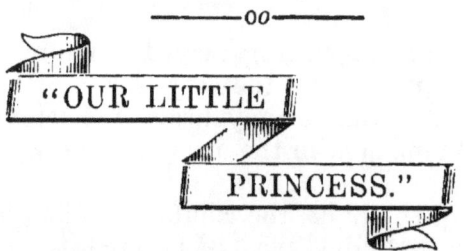

"Affection never is wasted."—LONGFELLOW.

FEAR not, oh gentlest heart that ever beat
　　In breast of woman—fear not thou to lay
The wealth of thy pure fondness at his feet,
　　For with a reverence deep he doth repay
Thee for the priceless gift that thou has given,
And at thy side he dreams of hope and Heaven.

He knows thy worth and goodness, and the light
　　As of a star-gemmed sky encircles thee,
With a strange glory all thy face is bright;
　　In spirit worship low he bends the knee,
And feels as if some seraph passing by
Paused in his flight to breathe a parting sigh.

Or as if some fair Princess from her throne
　　Stooped down to offer him a priceless gem
Plucked from her perfumed hair or dazzling zone;
　　He, daring not to touch her garment's hem,
Wishes that for her sake he were a king,
That he might claim the gift her white hands bring.

He walks beside thee, and he thinks some saint
　　Has stolen down to nestle at his heart,
His own with busy thought grows sick and faint,
　　He thinks of what he was and what thou art;
He looks into thine eyes, his own grow dim
With pitying tears, thou art too good for him.

Oh, that he were a monarch for thy sake,
　　To wrap thee in love's robe as in a dress;
Alas, the careless hand will lightly shake
　　The dew from off the flower, nor ever guess
That tho' in beauty's pride it rears its head,
Its morning freshness has for ever fled.

"Deceived, deceived," it is the sad refrain
　　Sung in its loneliness by many a life,
'Tis graven deep on many a throbbing brain;
　　"Deceived, deceived"—the doleful words are rife
With sad, stern meaning, like avenging fate,
Around our every path they stand and wait.

Like some pale Nemesis they haunt our bed,
　　They hover ghostlike by our fireside hearth,
In midnight's lonely hours, when all have fled
　　Who revelled round us in unthinking mirth;
A horrid phantom steals from out the gloom,
We feel its unseen presence in the room.

Ah, once, my girl, ah, once it was not so,
　　A boundless wealth of love was all his own;
He was deceived, and with one mighty throe,
　　One shuddering sigh, more sad than louder moan,
He saw his bark go down beneath the wave,
While 'bove the wreck grim furies wildly rave.

Bankrupt in love, he has no store to lay
　　In open-handed bounty at thy feet,
Yet when he basks beneath thine eyes' pure ray
　　His senses thrill with rapture wildly sweet;
Thou art so fair, so bright, that he is blest
To be in such a heart a passing guest.

Love on, fair child, enrich him with thy trust,
　　Thou wanderest now by fancy's fairy shore,
Too soon, alas, our idols turn to dust,
　　Such dreams as thine, once fled, return no more;
Therefore, be happy, thine the golden hours
When mercy veils the thorns beneath the flowers.

Think not thy fondness wasted, 'twill return
    Into thy generous breast a thousand fold—
O'er the unchanging past I fain would mourn,
    His was a nature cast in rarest mould;
Had he but known thee in that byegone time
Methinks I had no cause for this poor rhyme.

He would have worshipped thee, thou would'st have been
    An ever faithful guardian at his side,
Poor wearied soul—oh, keep this mem'ry green,
    Think of this love with fond, regretful pride;
Alas for her who blasted flowers and fruit,
And struck thy tree of promise at the root.

Farewell, sweet soul, I have no fears for thee,
    Thine unselfish nature brings its own reward;
Knowest thou not, girl, of that divinity
    Which hedges in and will for ever guard
A being fair and spotless as thou art—
Thy shield and buckler is thine own true heart.

It never can mislead thee—grief may come,
    Alas, it must come, 'tis our human fate;
But an Almighty Hand will line the gloom
    With rays of glory, and the glittering gate
Of hope and love will ope at thy behest,
And thou wilt enter into perfect rest.

And in the dim hereafter he will gaze
    Down the long vista of the past and see
Thy face love-lighted as in byegone days,
    Then will his worn heart breathe a prayer for thee,
While musing o'er the paths he with thee trod,
He'll walk more worthy Heaven and nearer God.

BROKEN VOWS.

YOU come to give me back my love, to ask me to restore
To you the pledge once to be mine till both our lives were o'er;
Oh, give me back my fond belief in human love and truth,
And give me back the sweet, bright dreams of innocence and youth;
Oh, give me back the trusting heart, the confidence of yore,
And give me back the undoubting faith that can return no more.

You give me back my vow and troth, but can you give to me
The simple faith, the hopeful trust that never more may be?
Can you recal to life and light the joy your words have slain?
Ah, no, for me life's unsoiled page will never ope again.

If others come to breathe the vows you whispered in my ear
With what distrust and bitter scorn shall I their story hear,
For I will think they also come to wound me and deceive,
No, tho' they swore by highest Heaven I could not them believe.

For once you swore your heart and love were mine, were only mine,
That when you changed the sun would cease in the blue heavens to shine,
And now you give me back my troth, you say your love is o'er,
You bid me to forget the past, to think of it no more.

Forget the past—oh, would to God I could the past forget,
Would I could fling you back your pledge and feel no vain regret;
But can I think of what you were, and what you now appear,
Without keen pangs of bitter grief, altho' I shed no tear?

Of what you were, my worshipped love, and, oh, what are you now?
False to yourself, false unto me, false to each plighted vow;
Yes, I must carry in my breast that sting you planted there,
And learn the hardest lesson taught—to suffer and to bear.

Yet, here's your pledge, I would not now you to your promise hold
For all the wealth of Shela's Queen, for all far India's gold;
I would not now, were you a king, be sharer of your throne,
Take back, take back your stained faith, my idol is o'erthrown.

———oo———

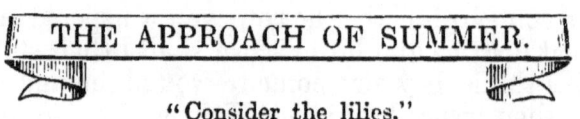

THE APPROACH OF SUMMER.

"Consider the lilies."

SUMMER is coming—from their long sleep waking,
   The flowers are bursting forth on hill and lea,
The wild bird soaring high, glad music making,
   Is telling of a Heaven we cannot see.

Summer is coming—the delightful story
   Is told by all the children of the wood,
From the tall oak, with branches grey and hoary,
   That all unmoved for centuries has stood,

Down to the slender willow, whose long tresses
    Bend gracefully to meet the murm'ring stream
That, rippling round its roots in soft caresses,
    Seems glad between its leaves to glance and gleam.

Summer is coming—on the verdant meadows
    Skip the white lambs, and on the daisied grass
We know her by the lengthening of the shadows
    And the low hum of insects as we pass.

Summer is coming—golden beams are stealing
    Athwart the azure skies at ev'ning time,
And stars at night seem little angels kneeling
    To peep thro' Heaven's curtains on our clime.

Summer is coming—every breath is laden
    With perfume borne to us by glittering seas,
And spring is ripening from a timid maiden
    Into a glorious woman born to please.

Hark to the tidings glad—lift hearts and voices
    Ye toiling children bowed by weary care,
When every living thing on earth rejoices
    Shall we, the sons of God, alone despair.

Shall we not act like men—'tis cowards only
    Who lie with craven faces in the dust,
What! if our lot be hard, our life's road lonely,
    Let us be strong and work, be brave and trust.

What if the cup be bitter—to my thinking
    No draught but has some sweetness in the bowl;
Let us then pledge our fate, and calmly drinking,
    Feel that it may not harm the living soul.

Is not this lesson taught us—morn still follows
    With all its gladsome train, the dreary night,
And though our path to-day is 'mong the hollows,
    To-morrow it may scale the mountain's height.

Out of the thunder-cloud the lightning starting
　　Makes glorious with its light the leaden skies,
And when the king of day is just departing
　　'Tis with a kingly pomp the monarch dies.

So should our hearts, when fainting 'neath earth's sorrow,
　　We fain would go to God in one long sigh,
From the day's death a bright example borrow,
　　And die like valiant men, if we must die.

After the winter's frost the glad stream rushing
　　On with rejoicing song now greets the sea,
So may we rend the chains our spirits crushing,
　　And know the glorious birthplace of the free.

Work while 'tis day—and your true souls possessing
　　The blessèd gift of patience, soon shall find
The load that was to earth your weak forms pressing
　　Had some good plan of God concealed behind.

We have despaired too long—too long have fainted,
　　Forgetting in our misery that He
Whose skilful finger every flower has painted,
　　Clothed every field and decked each forest tree,

Has us in His good keeping. If his tender kindness
　　Leaves not a flower unwaked from winter's death,
Is there not hope for us, whose mortal blindness
　　Makes us like those of old—" of little faith?"

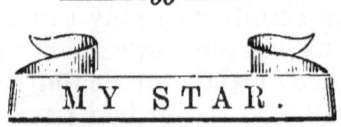

MY STAR.

THOU comest along my path to shine,
　　As stars upon the sea,
And if there's aught in me divine,
　　I caught the spark from thee.

I filled my empty cistern up
    At thy resplendent eyes,
And as I quaffed the brimming cup,
    I was both blest and wise.

Thine was the unseen hand which led
    Me from the brink of doom—
Thou wert the guiding star which shed
    Such radiance in the gloom.

And ever may thy holy light
    Illume life's troubled way,
Thou star, that in my darkest night
    Beamed with thy brightest ray.

When the big waves of dark despair
    Had risen like mountains high,
And murky clouds of grief and care,
    Were low'ring in the sky;

Piercing the gloom, I saw thee shine,
    With steady light on me,
And, oh! sweet star of joy be mine,
    I owe it all to thee.

LEONORE.

HERE is the spot I saw thee first,
    And here my faithful heart has nurst
        Dear thoughts of thee.
I wandered east, I wandered west,
But still thine image in my breast
        Unfaded yet must be.

A kiss has made it holy ground,
For never on the earth's wide bound,
  Such rapture have I known,
When as thy passion stood confest
I drew thee closer to my breast,
  And hailed thee as my own.

Thy face—it rises to me now—
The drooping eyes, the modest brow,
  The flitting blush
That stole across thy virgin cheek,
While neither dared with words to break
  Our souls' deep hush.

I went my weary way since then,
Amid the busy haunts of men
  I filled my place.
But not alone—thou still wert near,
Tho' thy dear voice I could not hear,
  Nor see thy face.

For me, sweet love, thou hast not died,
For thou wert ever at my side—
  Fair, as of old.
Oft have I turned me in my chair
And stretched my arms to empty air
  Thee to enfold.

I have one blessing in my life—
Thou know'st they gave to me a wife,
  And she has given
One child—a daughter—unto me,
And I have named her after thee
  My saint in Heaven.

Yes, I have called her by thy name;
Surely, my love, thou didst not blame
  My faithlessness.
Thou pitiest and forgave the sin,
For thou could see the void within
  They could not guess.

They thought me happy—and I tried
To smile on my unwelcome bride;
    But all in vain.
Then when a year had passed away,
And on her breast a baby lay,
    Death snapt the chain.

But she—my child,—I had almost said
Our child,—but we were all unwed—
    She knows my care,
And often when the fire burns low,
Her heart seems unto mine to grow,
    Her face to wear

An angel's beauty; while to me
She talks with rev'rent voice of thee,
    And bids me tell
How beautiful, and good, and true,
Was that sweet lady once I knew
    And loved so well.

Her name—I breathe it o'er and o'er
Thy name—my own lost Leonore.
    But yesternight
I spake it to myself, and she
Came gliding softly to my knee,
    With footsteps light.

"Father," my gentle darling said,
And on my bosom laid her head,
    And raised her eyes—
Her soft sad tearful eyes to mine;
Her eyes: nay love, I swear their thine,
    Blue as the skies,

With just the pleading tender look
Which first my heart a captive took,
    When long ago,
In our own native woods I felt,
My soul before thy presence melt,
    And to thee flow.

"Father," she said, and soft caressed
My hand in hers, and gently pressed
    To mine her cheek,
"There is one star which clearly, brightly
Burns at our chamber window nightly,
    It seems to speak

"Of that fair home, that blissful shore
Where dwells thine own lost Leonore;
    Oh, think that she
Is happy there," and then she raised
My face, and on the star we gazed
    She's given to thee.

I blessed her then my darling sweet,
For this her simple fond conceit,
    And evermore
At twilight hour, my child and I
Will search thy star out on the sky,
    My Leonore;

And looking on it I will think
That thou hast stolen to the brink
    Of thy fair land,
To gaze down on my earthly home,
And tho' thou may'st not, durst not come
    To clasp my hand,

Yet when thou seest my daughter's face,
All her sweet beauty and her grace,
    Thou wilt exclaim—
"One day I'll welcome him to Heaven,
Meantime a saint to him is given,
    Who bears my name."

THE GRAVE OF BALFE.

AS Erin wept her sainted son
    Passed from this world of weeping
To where—his work for mortals done—
    The harps of Heaven he's sweeping;
The goddess bright of song appearing,
Spake to her soul these words of cheering—

"Why weepest thou that men on earth
    Did not reward him rightly?
He's gone where angels know his worth,
    And where his crown glows brightly;
Now who would weep earth's gifts ungiven
When crowned by the hand of Heaven!

"Cheer thee and dry thy weeping eyes,
    Draw thy rent robe around thee,
Think from thy breast his life did rise,
    A mother true he found thee;
Thou gavest thy love—thou had'st no more,
And deathless is the name he bore.

"I have enrolled that tuneful name
    'Mid those of byegone glory,
Within the holiest niche of fame,
    To tell its undying story;
Hereafter when men speak his worth
I'll point them to his place of birth.

"'Twas Erin nursed his earliest years,
    'Twas Erin's bosom bore him,
His broken harp now dews with tears
    And the green turf that's o'er him;
With Erin is his name entwined,
And by my hand the link was joined.

"I sent this favorite of my train
  Awhile to glad and cheer thee,
But tho' I take him back again
  His spirit still is near thee;
Bind up thy dark, dishevelled hair,
And weep not in such wild despair.

"Has he not left his songs to thee
  To echo through all ages,
To make thine island of the sea
  Shine brighter on fame's pages?
And who would weep earth's gifts ungiven
Thus crowned by the hand of Heaven."

Then Erin rose and gently dried
  The tears she late was weeping,
On her soft cheek the flush of pride
  With sorrow's pallor keeping;
A rapid conflict—till a smile
Broke from her dewy eyes the while.

"I will not weep, my son," she said,
  "Tho' grief my life has shaded.
The crown you have placed upon his head
  Shall last thro' time unfaded;
And who would weep earth's gift ungiven
When crowned by the hand of Heaven."

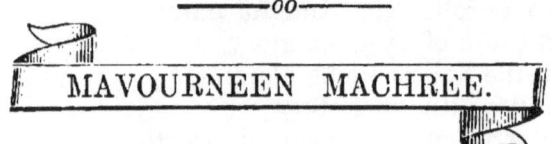

MAVOURNEEN MACHREE.

THERE is no land on earth so dear as the land we
  call our own.
There's no home like the old home, where life's best hours
  have flown,
And there's no love like the old love that round our hearts
  have grown,
    Mavourneen, mavourneen, mavourneen machree.

We travel far, we travel wide, and other lands we see,
We make us greater, grander homes, and newer loves have we,
But the old home and the old love are shrined in memory,
    Mavourneen, mavourneen, mavourneen machree.

They think I have forgotten you, but my heart is with you still,
Tho' you're lying far away in your grave so cold and chill,
And the memory of your tenderness my inmost soul can thrill,
    Mavourneen, mavourneen, mavourneen machree.

If I had robes of silken sheen and jewels for my hair,
If I had slaves to wait on me, could dine on dainties rare,
I'd spurn them all one little hour with you again to share,
    Mavourneen, mavourneen, mavourneen machree.

Oh, lonely is the world to me, since you, love, went away,
They blame me often for my tears, but how could I be gay;
Sure the very sun looks dim to me and all the sky is grey,
    Mavourneen, mavourneen, mavourneen machree.

Its not like summer to me now, e'en when the summer's here,
There's winter ever in my heart, and winter in the year,
It was not so when, long ago, you walked with me, my dear,
    Mavourneen, mavourneen, mavourneen machree.

Last week I saw a happy bride—oh, why is she so blest;
Come back from out your grave to me, and take me to your breast,
And give me back the last, last kiss that on your lips I prest,
    Mavourneen, mavourneen, mavourneen machree.

Oh, come and gather me again, close to your loving heart,
And wipe away these blinding tears that from my eyelids start,
Tell me 'twas all a horrid dream, and that we ne'er will part,
    Mavourneen, mavourneen, mavourneen machree.

Oh, there's no land on earth so dear as the land we call our own,
There's no home like the old home where life's best hours have flown,
And no love like the old love that with our growth has grown,
    Mavourneen, mavourneen, mavourneen machree.

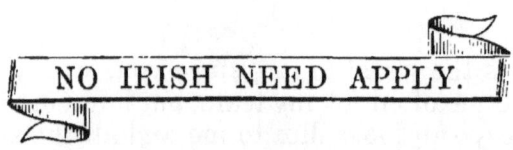

NO IRISH NEED APPLY.

SHAME on the lips that utter it, shame on the hands that write,
Shame on the page that publisheth such slander to the light;
I feel the blood with lightning speed, thro' all my veins fast fly,
At the old taunt, for ever new—No Irish need apply.

Are not our hands as stout and strong, our hearts as warm and true,
As their's, who fling this mock at us, to cheat us of our due?
While 'neath our feet God's earth stands firm, and o'er us hangs His sky,
Where there is honour to be won—The Irish need apply.

Oh, have not glorious things been done, by Irish hearts and hands ;
Is not our fame emblazoned far, o'er many seas and lands ?
There may be tears on Ireland's cheek, but still her heart beats high,
And where there's valour to be shown—The Irish need apply.

Wherever noble thoughts are nurst, and noble words are said—
Wherever patient endures, when hope itself seems dead—
Wherever honest industry, to win its goal will try—
Wherever manly toil prevails—The Irish need apply.

Wherever woman's love is pure, as is unsullied snow—
Wherever woman's cheek, at tales, of injury will glow—
Wherever pitying tears are shed, and breathed is feelings sigh—
Wherever kindliness is sought—The Irish need apply.

If there is aught of tenderness—if there is aught of worth—
If there's a trace of Heaven left, upon our sin-stained earth—
If there are noble steadfast hearts, that uncomplaining die,
To tread like them, life's thorny road—The Irish will apply.

Till on Killarney's waters blue, the soft stars cease to shine—
Till round the parent oak no more, the ivy loves to twine—
Till Nephin topples from his place, and Shannon's stream runs dry,
For all that's great and good and pure—The Irish will apply.

WOMAN'S RIGHTS.

IS it not woman's fate, to smother in
    Each soul-felt thought, each impulse of the heart;
To hide her love as 'twere a mortal sin—
    To act a careless, nay, unfeeling part.

E'en from her childhood is the lesson taught;
    She must not show her fondness, nor her hate—
She must not seek, she must herself be sought—
    She must be silent and in patience wait.

If but a word could bring her happiness,
    That word she dare not, ought not—will not speak;
All must be hid, and none may ever guess,
    Why is her eye so dim, so pale her cheek.

Men say their love is stronger; but I know
    A woman's self-control is greater far,
She sees her heart's desire, still come and go,
    As far from her as is the evening star.

She bids a cold "good morrow," while her breast
    Is all disturbed and quivering with her joy;
The love may grow apace, but ne'er confest
    She 'neath her mantle hides, the troublous boy.

Like to the fabled Spartan who of old
    Hid a fierce beast within his breast, nor gave
Sign of his agony, till chill and cold
    He sank, brave, patient soul, into the grave.

E'en so she smiles and smiles and presses down
    The anguish and the sickness of her soul,
For her the "world's dread laugh" or withering frown
    If once her o'erwrought feelings pass control.

She sees her loved one pass into death's gloom
    While her heart frights her with its yearning cry,
For her the flowers have lost their crimson bloom,
    And the warm light has faded from the sky.

And yet she bows her head and taketh up
    The cross of pain and goes her weary way,
Drinks, tho' with trembling lips, the bitter cup,
    And strives "Thy will be done" in faith to say.

Oh, woman! in thy weakness thou art strong,
    Oh, woman! in thy meekness thou art blest,
Sweet hopes and tender dreams to thee belong,
    The path of life by thee with flowers is drest.

We would not have thee seek a higher place
    Than that ordainéd thee by gracious Heaven—
The fireside hearth to gladden and to grace
    As comforter, consoler, wert thou given.

"Heaven's last, best gift wert thou," thy mission only
    To act with patience thine appointed part,
To speak the gentle word where sad and lonely
    And over-burdened beats some human heart.

To bless a husband's life, to cheer a brother,
    To be the light within a father's home,
Fond child, true sister, loving wife and mother,
    Thy task to chain with love what else might roam.

Such holy work is thine—by none disputed,
    These are thy "woman's rights," oh, cherish them;
Then shall each wayside flower thy hand has rooted
    Be in thy crown of life a fadeless gem.

A RETROSPECT—SOLD.

HOW thou comest to me, lost Alice,
    When my daily toil is done,
And I'm musing in the twilight
    By my silent hearth alone;
When to midnight ball and revel
    Troop the young, the fair, and gay,
And the voices and the footsteps
    Of the daylight's past away.

Then with head bowed on my bosom,
    And hands clasped upon my knee,
In the flickering, dying embers
    All the past I seem to see,
And the weight of years falls from me,
    While within my musing brain
Shadowy phantoms seem to hover,
    And the lost I see again.

Then with noiseless footsteps treading
    Through the half-closed open door
Comes the first love of my being
    In the happy days of yore,
Ere the world had come between us,
    And the glitter of his gold
Made her turn to my warm pleadings
    A careless ear and cold.

And again I see her standing
    In her father's stately home,
Again within the woodlands wide
    With her in thought I roam;
And a blush like lingering sunset
    Is glowing on her cheek,
And a smile that makes it radiant
    Beams upon me as I speak.

She breathes her vows with fervor,
　　She promises to be
My faithful love, my darling,
　　While life is left to me;
But those vows were long since broken,
　　Those words were all unsaid,
And the hopes which that morn budded
　　Are withered now and dead.

I wonder is she happy now
　　With the husband of her choice,
I loved her so, my spirit
　　At her pleasure could rejoice.
Yet they tell me she is paler
　　And thinner than of old,
Some whisper that for money
　　Her peace of mind was sold,

And that she for whose soft bidding
　　My life I'd once laid down
Is but reaping bitter harvest
　　From seed herself has sown.
They say her witching beauty
　　Has begun to droop and fade,
That to fairer, fresher faces
　　His homage now is paid.

While she seldom looks and coldly
　　On her fair, unconscious child,
And that never by its prattling
　　Is her loneliness beguiled.
That her once bright eyes are heavy
　　With tears in secret shed,
And that she I almost worshipped
　　In heart and soul is dead.

Oh, lost love of my boyhood,
　　Had'st thou been true to me,
Had the babe that calls thee "Mother"
　　But climbed upon my knee

I'd not be sitting lonely
  By my silent hearth to-night,
And thine eyes would be less heavy
  And thy soft cheek be less white.

ELEANORE'S PICTURE.

I FAIN would paint thy picture, but my hand
    Drops useless down. I cannot paint aright,
As on the brink of some clear stream I stand,
  To catch from its soft breast the varying light,
Oh, for a magic pencil, my best friend,
To paint a life in which all virtues blend.

E'enwhile one sang of thee in loving words,
  And our hearts echoed to the tender strain,
'Twas with a skilful hand he swept the chords;
  In poesy's cloud-palace some souls reign,
While others only serve—wake silent lute,
My heart o'erflows altho' my tongue be mute.

Our "sweet Aunt Nelly," 'tis by that dear name
  We must for evermore remember thee—
Justly our tenderest memory dost thou claim;
  Must the days come when we no more shall see
Thy kind eyes bid us welcome at the door,
Fain would we keep thee with us, Eleanore.

Few, few like to thyself are left behind,
  I look around in vain thy peer to seek,
Who was so tender (wise, so thoughtful) kind,
  I cannot help these tears upon my cheek;
A precious link wert thou in my life's chain,
Where shall I find a friend like thee again.

Older than thou, I ever looked to thee
  For counsel and for comfort in distress,
Oft when my blinded eyes no light could see
  I've learned from thee to praise, to hope, to bless,
And in thy soothing words there lay such balm
The troubled waves were stilled, and all was calm.

Ah me, when I bethink me of our walks,
  Our pleasant wanderings in the sunny noon,
Thy snatches of sweet song, our fireside talks,
  Now gay, now solemn, like some tender tune
Learned in our youth—forgotten, nevermore
Come memories of thee, loved Eleanore.

Friend of my youth—oh, it is hard to let
  The few who love us from our pathway glide;
But thou, tho' we are parted, ne'er forget
  In the dim, shadowy future yet untried,
That, graven deep within our bosoms' core,
Thy cherished name is found, my Eleanore.

———oo———

THE SPECTRE BRIDEGROOM.

MY heart o'erfloweth to mine eyes,
  And my tears flow down like rain,
When I think of the love that is gone for aye,
  That ne'er shall be mine again,
When I think of the dreams I used to dream,
  Of the hopes that all were vain.

My heart o'erfloweth to mine eyes
  When I think of auld lang syne,
And the cup that was once so strangely sweet
  Tastes bitter and salt as brine;
Ah, nought but the lees are left me now,
  God's hand spilt the rich red wine.

The cup of pain I drain it deep,
  There is wormwood on the brim,
There is fennel floating dark below,
  Oh, God! how my eyeballs swim;
What is this stealing to my side?
  'Tis a spectre stern and grim.

"There's a dark, dark stain on your brow, my love,
   A stain of the red, red mould,
These are not the arms that oft of yore
   My waist would close enfold,
And the lips that clung warm and soft to mine
   Are icy, icy cold.

"Are these the kisses you used to give
   In the bonny woods long ago,
When we watched the lazy cloudlets sail
   O'er the sky-fields to and fro,
When we paused by the rippling river's brink
   To list to its tuneful flow.

Why are your lips so cold, so cold,
   I feel no quivering breath,
Can you not rest in your quiet bed,
   The waving grass beneath?"
"I have stolen awhile from the churchyard's gloom,
   From the dark domain of death.

"I cannot rest in my narrow bed,
   'Tis dark and I'm alone,
Why do you shrink so from my kiss—
   On earth were you not my own;
Ah, you're grown paler now than you used to be,
   And your cheek has thinner grown.

"Do you think of the wide old window seat
   In the old house far away,
When together we gazed on the purple peaks
   Blush red at the close of day,
Ere they silently sank to their shadowy sleep
   In the summer twilight grey.

"Oh, the sweet old songs you used to sing
   As we stood by the salt sea waves,
I hear them still at the midnight hour
   Sighing softly o'er the graves,
With a mournful sound like the distant dash
   Of ocean in its caves.

"Do you think of the nights we used to stand
  And watch the pale stars shine,
When closer and closer round my neck
  Your arms you would fond entwine;
Nay, turn not so from my clasp away,
  Your lips—are they not mine.

"Ere long, ere long I must hie me back
  To the place where worms creep,
Oh, say will you come with me, my love,
  And share my dreamless sleep,
Our bridal bed may be cold and chill,
  But our rest will be calm and deep?

"At crow of cock I must return,
  Say will you share my bed?"
Then he kissed her lips with a greedy kiss,
  And with a groan he fled;
But when morning dawned they found her lie
  All stiff and stark and dead.

―――oo―――

THE BALLAD OF EFFIE BURTON.

EFFIE, lay aside thy broidery, I would speak alone
    with thee,
Look, the sun is almost sinking to his rest within the sea,
And I must be on the billow ere the dawn is in the skies,
I have much to tell you, cousin, heavy on my heart it lies.

Rushed the red blood to her forehead, bathing all the
    downcast face,
And she rose to give him answer with a woman's gentle
    grace,
In my father's quiet garden stands my favorite linden tree,
On the rustic bench beneath it I will sit and talk with thee.

Effie, long before I knew you, when with blessing life was stored,
There was one on whom I doted, whom my inmost soul adored,
She—but ah, I will not name her—it is written on my worb
What her treachery has made me, but I will not curse her now,
For her heart was pure and sinless till the wily tempter came
From the paths of peace to lure her to a deep abyss of shame;
I had wooed her, I had wed her, laid the glory of my life
At the feet of her trusted—perjured woman, faithless wife,
'Twas one morn as I lay sleeping that she stole out from my side,
Need I wound thy gentle bosom—by this hand the spoiler died.
Is it for the crime, sweet Effie, that those tender tears you weep?
Know you not revenge is precious, and my wrongs were foul and deep;
Think not, cousin, that I slew him with the base assassin's knife,
No, it was in open combat that I took away his life.
From that hour I did not see her, but they tell me that within
The deep cloister's stern seclusion made she penance for her sin,
That by sorrow, worn and wasted, stung by anguish and remorse,
Ere the year had flown they found her in the cold grey dawn a corpse.
Cursed and wretched, sick and weary, maddened by my heart's deep pain,
Fled I from my sullied hearthstone far across the trackless main,
Over land and sea I wandered until fainting, sick and poor,
You, my gentle cousin, found me lying at your father's door.
Thick the snow lay on the threshold, these old trees looked grim and bare,

And you seemed like some good angel sent down from the realms of air,
O'er me then you bent and lifted from the snow-clad earth my head,
And I felt the tears of pity that for me you freely shed,
Like the blessèd dew of Heaven fell they on my burning brain,
And methinks each bright drop lightened the deep burden of my pain;
Then your kind old father led me to the comfort of his hearth,
Asked me of my name and lineage, bade me tell my place of birth,
And when I my name repeated, with a gladsome voice he cried—
" Oh, my sister's son, my nephew, with us evermore abide."
Then beneath your quiet rooftree, found I peace and rest at last;
For your gentle kindness led me from the agonizing past,
And tho' e'en the name of woman, had been loathsome unto me,
Yet I would be more than human, thus to think, and look on thee.
Yes, tho' seared in heart and blighted, I can love and trust once more,
Knowing this, I now must leave you, tho' the struggle will be sore;
You could never look with fondness, on a wretch so lorn as I;
Oh, forgive me! that I pain you, that I make you thus to sigh.
Never shall I curse you, Effie, with a love so sad as mine,
If my own life has been clouded, wherefore cast a gloom o'er thine;
Fare thee well my gentle cousin—turn not thus your face away—
Let my sad fate be remembered, when your nightly prayer you pray;
And when years have passed, my Effie, when sweet children climb your knee,

And you call another "husband"—oh, with pity think of me.
Then arose fair Effie Burton, lifted up her drooping head,
While her soft cheek, flushed and faded, in the stillness
  thus she said—
"Richard, since the day I found you, now six happy
  months, and more,
In the chilly wintry evening, lying at my father's door;
Since that blessed hour, dear Richard, I have loved but
  you alone—
If you prize my heart's devotion, it has long been all your
  own."

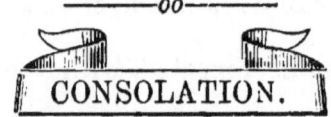

CONSOLATION.

OH, say not the swallows will come no more,
  They've but skimmed the purple sea,
They will build 'neath your eaves, when the budding leaves
  Are decking each forest tree.
Say not the flowers are cold and dead,
  They're but buried 'neath the snow,
And they will arise, when from azure skies,
  The balmy breezes blow.
Say not the light of the sun is quenched,
  By yon driving thunder cloud;
He yet will shine, with his light divine,
  From behind his sable shroud.

And oh, when thy Maker hides His face
  Say not thou art forgot;
He but waits awhile upon thee to smile—
  But, ah, He forgets thee not.
'Tis the fogs and mists of our own dear isle,
  That makes her turf so green;
So 'neath mountains of cares, and thro' mists of tears,
  Are hearts of emerald seen.
This weary waiting, but tries our faith,
  For the promise in patience wait,
Though it tarry long—let our hope be strong—
  It can never come too late.

IDA'S FAITH.

"Love is strong as death."

[Taken from a legend told by Lord Lytton, in "The Pilgrims of the Rhine."]

THE angels swept their harps in Heaven,
    Their notes like perfumed air,
And the harp of the angel Seralim,
    Made the sweetest music there.

From the throne came forth, the Mighty Voice,
    Of Him no eye can see,
And He spake to the Angel Seralim—
    "Ask thou a boon of me."

"There's a star : 'tis a place of torturing
    Where the souls of many dwell,
'Tis the painful porch of our glorious Heaven—
    'Tis the one escape from hell.

"There be many there, who worship Thee,
    Yet faint 'neath tortures dire ;
Grant me the boon, to visit them,
    And soothe them with my lyre,"

The voice replied—"Thy prayer is heard :
    Go gentlest angel, go
Touch thy sweet harp, if its tender strains
    Can mitigate their woe."

The angel entered the crystal gates
    And folding his snowy wings,
With skilful hand he touched his lyre,
    And swept its golden strings.

Then peace on the wretched seemed to fall,
   Yet one wail the wide hall crost—
" Oh Adenheim, Adenheim," said the voice,
   " Mourn not the loved and lost."

The angel struck chord after chord,
   But still the cry arose ;
Wondering, he questioned, " whose was the soul,
   That could not know repose ?"

'Twas the soul of a woman, young and fair,
   That poured this plaintive cry,
Chained to a rock, while demons grim,
   Were standing idle by.

" Does the song I sing, lull even ye
   Foul torturers to rest ?"
And they said, " Our torments are not so great
   As the anguish in her breast."

" Wherefore, O daughter, dost thou mourn
   With such a plaintive wail,
Why is the song that soothes the rest
   To thee of no avail ?"

" Oh stranger, beautiful and bright,
   Thou seest before thee one,
Who on the earth loved the creature more,
   Than the dweller on Heaven's throne.

" My torment is just—but my Adenheim,
   Mourns ceaselessly for me,
And the thought of his grief, is greater pain
   Than these fiery tortures be."

" And how knowest thou he mourns thee thus
   " Because," the spirit cried,
" Thus I would have mourned my Adenheim,
   If he before me died."

The heart of the gentle angel thrilled,
　"How can I ease thy pain?"
"Give me, oh give me, to visit earth—
　To see his face again."

"I would grant thy boon, but the penalty
　To visit earth is great,
Thou must linger here still a thousand years—
　'Tis too terrible a fate."

"Willingly" then the spirit cried,
　"The doom thou fearest, I'll brave;
Ages of torture I'll endure,
　One hour from him to save."

And the spirit stretching her shadowy arms,
　Pleaded so piteously,
That the angel opened the barred gates
　And set the mourner free.

* * * * * * * *

It was night in the halls of Adenheim,
　And dressed in robes of state—
His vassals round—the lord of the feast,
　In pomp and power sate,

And one who was fairer than the moon,
　Sat his chair of state beside;
'Twas the noble dame of Falkenberg,
　He wooed to be his bride.

"Thy words of love, Lord Adenheim,
　What lady can believe—
Did not Loden's maidens, a wedding crown
　For the brows of Ida weave?

"And scarce three little months have past,
  Till thou plightest me the same—
The blush that is rising on my cheek
  Is less of love than shame."

"By my halidom," quoth Lord Adenheim,
  "Thou doest thy beauty wrong;
Love Ida—nay, thou mockest me,
  I did not love *her* long.

"A few gay words—a few bright smiles—
  Behold the love I bore!
No; trust me, fair dame of Falkenberg,
  I never loved before."

He ceased, and a faint sad sigh he heard
  Behind his golden chair,
He turned to see but a misty cloud,
  That vanished into air.

"Was it for this," quoth Seralim,
  "Thou hast added years of pain,
For a thousand more in these painful halls
  Thy spirit must remain?"

"Alas! after what I endured on earth,
  What are those years to me,
The suffering there, in one little hour,
  Was an eternity!"

EDITH'S SACRIFICE.

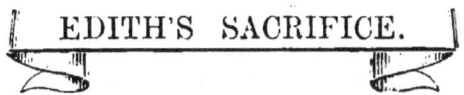

"From a scene in Lord Lytton's "Harold."

COME, sweet harp, and let me tune thee
    To a wild and mournful lay,
Let me sing of days departed,
    And of ages passed away.

Sing of him, the great and noble,
    Who for freedom bled and died,
Seventh son of great Earl Godwin—
    England's glory and her pride.

Sing of her, the true and faithful,
    Half a woman, half a saint;
All of earth that's pure and lovely,
    Yet without one early taint.

She who gave up all we cherish,
    All we value most in life—
Love and hope and joy unbounded,
    And the sweet, sweet title—wife.

Ere within her golden tresses
    Time had sown one thread of grey,
When the pulse of youth was bounding,
    And life seemed one holiday.

In that hour when passion pleadeth,
    And the heart beats loud and high,
On the altar of fair freedom
    Did her true heart bleed and die.

*   *   *   *   *   *

In her chamber sat the maiden—
    Sat and dreamed she of her love,
And the sunbeams were not brighter
    Than the dreams her fancy wove.

She was 'neath her husband's roof-tree,
    Played her children round her knee,
Happy wife and happy mother—
    Who on earth so blest as she?

When he late had kissed her forehead
    He had bidden her have no fear;
All the toil at last was over,
    He had made the pathway clear.

Hark! a footstep—scarce joy's tear-drops
    On her soft, fair cheek are dried,
When she sees with mute amazement
    Priest and warrior by her side.

Thrilled her heart with nameless terror,
    Had some sorrow fallen on him?
And she rose and turned upon them
    Eyes with fear and loving dim.

"Daughter, we have come to ask thee
    Wilt thou save our native land?
Choose between thy love and England—
    Girl, our fate is in thine hand!

"If Earl Harold weds thee, Edith,
    Nought can this poor country save,
And our fair, our lovely England,
    Will be one wide, yawning grave.

"Aldyth, with her stout retainers,
    Ready waits to be his bride,
And, with all her trusty spearmen,
    E'en the Norman is defied.

"And the people wait to crown him
  King of this fair isle, if he—
May God comfort thee, my daughter;
  Yes, thou know'st it—gives up thee.

"Ah, poor heart! thou can'st not do it,
  But for this great sacrifice,
Think, a heavenly crown awaits thee,
  In the mansions of the skies."

Thrice she spoke, but vain the effort,
  Nothing could her lips reply,
And they read the mute inquiry
  In the wildly mournful eye.

Then outspake the warrior stately—
  "Edith, cousin, thinkest thou
That *he* sent us thus to wound thee
  By my knightly faith, not so!

"He will ne'er resign thee, Edith,
  Tho' it be for England's sake,
And the ties that bind thee to him
  Thou alone on earth can break."

Flushed her cheek—and one short moment
  To her love and hope she gave,
Then she cried, "Oh, Harold, hear me,
  'Tis our own loved land to save.

"All is over, ye have conquered—
  To him still this heart may cling;
But he ne'er shall wed with Edith—
  Go and hail him England's King."

DEAN KIRWAN'S LAST CHARITY SERMON.

A SEA of faces, fixed on one grey head
    That rose like some old lighthouse 'mid the crowd;
He looked around, yet never word he said,
    But o'er his snowy 'kerchief calmly bowed,
Then turned, and with a look of love and woe
Gazed on the orphan group who knelt below.

He took the white cloth slowly from his face,
    And lo! 'twas reddened with his true heart's blood;
Then, with a gesture like a fond embrace,
    He bent him o'er the babes that nigh him stood,
And lifting up to Heaven his agèd head,
"Oh, my poor children," with a groan, he said.

It was enough, the anguish of that tone,
    The mute imploring of that gesture mild—
His heart's blood he had given, his work was done,
    He leaves to others now each orphan child.
They bore him to his bed with weeping eyes,
From which the soldier worn, no more may rise.

But that dyed 'kerchief and that anguished cry,
    That "oh, my children," echoed in each soul,
Out of their gifts men gave abundantly,
    And few their mournful sobbings could control;
And all went forth with meekness and with awe
To tell their children's children what they saw.

Still is the scene remembered, still warm tears
    Are loosened from their sources by the tale,
That "oh, my children," echoes thro' all years,
    That bubbling life-stream bids the cheek grow pale;
Still is his mem'ry hallowed, and his tomb
Is hung with garlands that for aye shall bloom.

THE TURNING OF THE TIDE.

FEW the joys and many sorrows
    That our lot in life divide,
And from youth to age we're waiting
    For the turning of the tide.

Ever hoping that the morrow
    Will some blessèd tidings bring
To uproot a rooted sorrow,
    To pluck out some secret sting.

Ever hoping that the future
    Will be brighter than the past:
That our night is nearly over,
    That the day must dawn at last.

Up the steep we've long been toiling,
    And the top we soon must gain;
Yet, when we have reached the summit,
    'Tis to find our hopes were vain.

For a higher peak is looming
    In the distance far away,
And the pathway grows more rugged,
    And the shadowy clouds more grey.

On the beach of time we're standing,
    Watching for the tide to turn,
Till Death's pitying angel leads us
    Softly o'er the silent bourne.

Oh! that to our Heavenly Father
    We could all our cares confide,
And with faith and hope and patience
    Wait the turning of the tide.

CHANCE MEETINGS.

AS thro' the night we're going,
   How pleasant 'tis to find
A star, its bright face showing,
   Tho' daylight's left behind;
And now and then, when keeping
   Our lonely vigils, we
Feel all our pulses leaping
   Its welcome light to see.

So as thro' life we're taking
   Perchance our weary way,
Our pleasant paths forsaking,
   Our rosy clouds turned grey;
'Tis pleasant kindly faces
   To meet e'en for a while,
To see the warm heart's traces
   Within the kindly smile.

We know the cup we're drinking
   Will pass us by-and-bye,
And yet each moment's linking
   Our hearts by mem'ry's tie.
Time passes, swiftly fleeing—
   We own the spirit's spell;
Touch hands in friendly greeting,
   Then grasp them in farewell.

So airs from Heaven drove thee
   A moment in my way,
My spirit fain would love thee—
   Yet knows thee but a day.
My fancy e'en now lingers
   Upon thy fair girl face,
I clasp thy soft, warm fingers,
   And mark thy artless grace.

Thou'lt go, and I may never
  Behold thy face again!
The air-spun cord will sever
  As snow dissolves in rain;
But still the gold hair shining
  Above thine open brow
Shall round my thoughts be twining
  Ev'n as it twineth now.

A child, and yet a woman—
  Never the charm resign;
The heavenly and the human
  Are blent in souls like thine.
Be still a child in spirit
  When years have passed o'er thee:
'Tis woman's chiefest merit
  Guileless and fond to be.

May all love ever hold thee,
  May all love ever bless,
The kindest doth enfold thee
  Now as in long caress;
With it, except the blessing
  A stranger sends in this,
Nor chide her frank confessing
  If she has done amiss.

A FRIENDLY GREETING.

FRIENDS, tho' I may ne'er behold you,
   Never clasp your hands in mine,
Yet my spirit arms enfold you,
   And around you mem'ries twine—
Tender mem'ries that shall never
   Fade or perish from my heart;
Bound by links no time can sever,
   Ye are of my past a part.

Ye have writ your name in kindness
   Deep within an anguished breast,
Mourned a sick soul's moaning blindness,
   And its agonising guest.
Tears the angels now are weeping
   Were the tears your kind eyes shed
O'er the worn out heart that's sleeping
   Calmly with its kindred dead.

Love and death with hands enfolden
   Draw you ever to my side—
Mine a story sad and olden,
   Yours a friendship true and tried;
Oft my fancy now shall wander
   To your city by the sea,
Oft my dreaming heart shall ponder
   O'er your tenderness for me.
And tho' I may ne'er behold you—
   Never clasp your hands in mine,
Yet my spirit arms enfold you,
   And around you mem'ries twine.

Dublin: Printed by W. J. ALLEY & Co., Ryder's Row, Capel St.

ERRATA.

Allan and Bessie—Page 33, verse 4, 1st line, for "jessamine" read "jasmine." page 35, verse 8 (part II.), 4th line, for "only" read "favorite."

Blind Man's Bride—Page 44, verse 3, 3rd line, for "these" read "thee."

Maclise's Last Painting—Page 53, last verse, 3rd line, for "spake" read "speaks."

In Memoriam—Page 53, "In Memori*u*m" should be "In Memoriam."

An Old Song—Page 76, verse 6, 1st line, for "wringing" read "winging," and in page 81, verse 2, 6th line, for "wing" read "wring."

On K. weeping—Page 96, "on R. weeping" should be "on K. weeping."

Væ Victis—Page 98, "Vae Victis" should be "Væ Victis."

An Invocation—Page 106, last verse, 2nd line for "I'll lay down my head," should be "I'll lay my head down."

Muses' Defence—Page 122, verse 2, 2nd line, for "looks" read "look ;" page 124, verse 11, for "binds" read "bind."

Devil's Holiday—Page 125, verse 9, 4th line, for "heart" read "hearth."

No Irish Need Apply—Page 167, verse 4, 2nd line, the word "faith" is left out after "patient."

Approach of Summer—Page 158, verse 13, 4th line, for "birthplace" read "birthright."

www.ingramcontent.com/pod-product-compliance
Lightning Source LLC
Chambersburg PA
CBHW020843160426
43192CB00007B/759